Ribbonwork *Flowers*

Christen Brown

132 Garden Embellishments

Beautiful Designs for Flowers, Leaves & More

C&T PUBLISHING

Text copyright © 2015 by Christen Brown

Photography and artwork copyright © 2015 by C&T Publishing, Inc.

Publisher: Amy Marson

Creative Director: Gailen Runge

Art Director / Cover Designer: Kristy Zacharias

Editors: Liz Aneloski and Lee Jonsson

Technical Editor: Ellen Pahl

Book Designer: Christina Jarumay Fox

Production Coordinator: Jenny Davis

Production Editor: Katie Van Amburg

Illustrator: Valyrie Gillum

Photo Assistant: Mary Peyton Peppo

Instructional photography by Christen Brown; Project photography by Diane Pedersen, unless otherwise noted

Published by C&T Publishing, Inc., P.O. Box 1456, Lafayette, CA 94549

Library of Congress Cataloging-in-Publication Data

Brown, Christen (Christen Joan)

Ribbonwork flowers : 132 Garden embellishments--beautiful designs for flowers, leaves & more / Christen Brown.

     pages cm

ISBN 978-1-61745-015-0 (softcover)

1. Ribbon work. 2. Ribbon flowers. I. Title.

TT850.5.B758 2015

746--dc23

                              2014029600

Printed in China

10 9 8 7 6 5 4 3 2 1

HAPPY CREATING

I dedicate this book to all my students, both past and present. Thank you for giving me this opportunity to share my knowledge with you. May you always find the time to enjoy the creative adventure.

With love to you all,

Christen

Heart's Desire,
3½″ × 3⅜″

Red and
White Vase,
3″ × 6¾″

Flower Child,
5½″ × 6″

MY BIGGEST FANS

*To my husband, Kevin, and daughter, Gwen,
thank you for your unconditional love and
support and allowing me to play in my room.
Love you!*

SPECIAL
ACKNOWLEDGMENTS

*I have been fortunate to have the most
wonderful people helping me throughout
the process of designing, writing, editing,
and photographing this book. I would like
to thank each and every person whose
expertise has touched these pages. Special
thanks go to Liz, my editor, who has been
with me for each book; you know how
special you are, and I do appreciate you.*

CONTENTS

VISUAL GUIDE

BEGINNING FLOWERS... 23

25
Rosette

29
Boat Gather Petals

34
Folded Petals

26
Posy

30
Gather and Grab Petals

35
Gathered Loop Petals

27
Knotted Posy and
Knotted Ruffled Posy

31
Gala Gather Petals

36
Ruched Petals

28
Double Posy and Fancy
Rosette or Posy

32
Hop 'n Stitch Petals

37
Crinkle Fold Petals

33
Star Point Petals

38
Flip 'n Fold Petals

VINTAGE FLOWERS... 39

41
Rosie Mantle

45
Calla Lily

49
Windflower

42
Gazania

46
Heliotrope

50
Petunia

43
Cassiope

47
Cymbidium

51
Pansy

44
Sweetheart's Flower

48
Primrose

52
Queen's Climber

MINSTREL'S FLOWERS ... 53

Nemesia
55

Yarrow
61

Hydrangea
56

Flowering Quince
62

Amaryllis
57

Irish Rose
63

Cockle Shells
58

Wild Rose
64

Cup and Saucer Vine
59

Columbine
65

Day Lily
60

Larkspur
66

SUMMER FLOWERS ... 67

Double Daisy
69

Grand Duchess
75

Angel Wing Begonia
70

Campion
76

Sweet Alyssum
71

Impatiens
77

Estrella with Silk Center
72

Rosie Rambler
78

Pennine Mum
73

Empress Lily
79

Chrysanthemum
74

Pincushion Flower and Pincushion Center
80

BOHEMIAN FLOWERS ... 81

Hibiscus
83

Passion Flower
89

Moulin Rouge
84

Ballerina Fuchsia
90

Gypsy Dandelion
85

Lily of the Valley
91

Puck's Rose
86

Court Jester
92

Spanish Dancer
87

Royal Dahlia
93

Orchid
88

Claire de Lune
94

Elegant Flowers ... 95

97

Gentle Lady

98

English Miss

99

Petite Bud

99

Silk Bloom

100

Chou Rose

101

Fontana Rose

102

Saucy Miss

103

Pompom Rose

104

Symphony Rose

105

Guinevere's Rose

106

Vintage Favorite

108

Romantic Rose

Petals, Leaves, and Greenery ... 109

111

Prairie Point Leaf or Petal

111

Soft Curve Leaf or Petal

112

Simple Leaf or Petal

112

Loop Leaf or Petal

113

Pinch Tip Leaf or Petal

113

Box Fold Leaf or Petal

114

Rooftop Leaf or Petal

114

Bandana Fold Leaf or Petal

115

Slender Tip Leaf or Petal

115

Miter Fold Leaf or Petal

116

Simple Flower

117

Renaissance Leaf

117

Sweet Leaf

118

Deco Leaf

118

Neapolitan Leaf

119

Art Nouveau Leaf

119

Ruched Leaf

120

Oval Leaf

120

Notched Leaf

121

Frilly Leaf

121

Ivy Leaf

122

Baroque Leaf

122

Tuxedo Fold Leaf

123
Winged Leaf

125
Cord stem or ribbon stem

128
Single or Double Knot

131
Berry and Stuffed Berry

135
Pretty Lady

138
Apple

123
Hooded Leaf

126
Wire stem

128
Jelly Roll Center

132
Pouf Gather Center

138
Snail

135
Cherry

124
Bow Tie Leaf

126
Wire tendril

129
Ruffled Rosette and Double Rosette

132
Stamens

136
Ladybug

139
Swallowtail Butterfly

124
Figure 8 Leaf

130
Rose Bud Center

133
French Knot

136
Grape Bunch

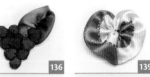

139
Frilly Heart

130
Rose Hips

133
Buttons

137
Peapod

140
Strawberry

DOWN THE
Garden Path

My grandparents' garden was truly a delight to behold and my secret pleasure. It was filled with colorfully arranged, delicate plants that bloomed throughout the spring and summer. My love of color was ignited and enriched by this treasured garden and by the wildflowers that grew in the open fields around our cottage in the Canadian countryside. I often filled an old porcelain pitcher we found at a flea market with huge bouquets of flowers, greenery, and delicate ferns. I thought then—and still do now—how grand!

A Bag Full of Ribbons

Growing up with a mom who sewed her children's wardrobes was common during the 1960s. My mom made matching outfits for herself, my sister, and me, and with the leftover fabric she made sure our Barbies all had fabulous duds too! As a kid, I remember saving up the package labels from the bindings and trims that she used, to send back to the manufacturer.

In return, we would receive a bag full of odd bits of ribbons and lace. I learned how to make my first ribbonwork flower, the Rosette, from the directions provided in one of those "goodie" packets.

Vintage vase full of Rosette flowers

Petals and Posies

When I first began teaching, I primarily focused on wearable art and dollmaking classes. One of my students asked me to teach her how to make ribbon-work flowers, and so I created a series of classes that I called Petals and Posies. These were my first ribbon-work classes, with many of the ideas based on vintage flowers and techniques I had developed.

Group of French wire and woven ribbon corsages

Ribbonwork vs. Ribbon Embroidery

I have found through my years as a teacher that some clarification is necessary when describing rib-bonwork and ribbon embroidery. The two are often referred to interchangeably, but in actuality each follows a different technique and uses different needles and materials.

Ribbon embroidery is threading the needle with the ribbon and stitching through fabric to form a flower, leaf, or other design, which enhances the surface of the fabric.

Ribbonwork is stitching a length of ribbon with needle and thread to form a flower, leaf, or other design, as a separate, individual unit.

Summer Tea, 4″ × 2½″ deep; ribbonwork Rosettes glued to crochet teacup

Sunflower, 3⅞″ × 5″; ribbonwork flower with center embroidered with silk ribbon

Paisley Brooch, 3¼″ × 1⅞″; ribbon embroidery worked on pin, made from cotton fabric

a special note

As with my first book, *Ribbonwork Gardens*, I have designed a wide variety of flowers, leaves, and garden accessories using basic techniques. Many of these designs include references to specific directions that have been explained and illustrated on another page. If ribbonwork is new to you or you need a refresher course, I suggest you read through the next two chapters, as well as Getting Down to Basics (page 141) and Terms, Tools, and Tips (page 146).

RIBBONS AND LACE

Sweet Wreath, 5"

Your Flower Garden

The flowers I have included in this book are stylized versions of real flowers, plus a few that are merely my fantasy. In each of the flower chapters I have grouped flowers for presentation purposes only. Feel free to mix it up, so to speak, and create a bouquet of your own.

A Variety of Ribbons

Ribbons

The three types of ribbon you will use to create the ribbonwork designs in this book are silk bias, wire-edge, and woven ribbons. Silk bias ribbons are made from silk fabric that is cut on the bias. Wire-edge ribbons are made with a fine wire woven into the selvage edges. Woven ribbons are made from a variety of fiber contents with finished selvage edges.

SILK BIAS RIBBON

Silk bias ribbon is cut on the bias from silk fabric, which provides a subtle drape. The ribbon has raw edges along the width and a stitched seam about every 2 yards.

1. Flowering Quince; 2. English Miss; 3. Primrose

- Silk habotai has a soft hand and a slightly dull finish and is double-sided.

- Silk satin has a soft hand and is shiny on one side and dull on the other.

- Silk velvet has a soft to medium hand and has a soft and plush finish on one side and a flat and dull finish on the other.

WIRE-EDGE RIBBON

Amaryllis and Gentle Lady

French wire ribbon and wire-edge ribbon are usually made from a fine woven taffeta ribbon with a thin wire sewn through the selvage edges. The hand is usually medium, depending on the fiber content.

WOVEN RIBBON

Woven ribbons come in a variety of fiber contents, weaves, textures, surfaces, and hands; all have a finished selvage edge.

1. Queen's Climber; 2. Symphony Rose; 3. Rosette; 4. Gala Gather Petal Flower;
5. Boat Gather Petal Flower; 6. Vintage Favorite; 7. Double Daisy Variation;
8. Sweetheart's Flower; 9. Folded Petal Flower; 10. Star Point Petal Flower; 11. Posy

1. Double-sided satin comes with a shiny finish on both sides, often with a different color on each side. The hand is soft to stiff, depending on the fiber content.

2. Grosgrain ribbons are woven with a pattern of raised ribs of thread that run through the width of the ribbon. Petersham grosgrain ribbon has a scalloped selvage edge that is created during the weaving process. The hand is medium to stiff due to the fiber content and weave.

3. Jacquard refers to the complex overshot pattern of threads that are woven to resemble an embroidered pattern on the right side of the ribbon. The hand is medium to stiff due to the weave.

4. The picot or ruffled edge of a novelty ribbon will always be the outer edge of a design. A woven ribbon with a pleated, folded, or textured surface will render a right or wrong side of the ribbon. The hand will depend on the type of ribbon and can be soft to stiff.

5. Rayon hem tape is a soft, loosely woven ribbon with a supple drape. The hand is soft due to the fiber content.

6. Organza, georgette, and organdy are sheer ribbons that are often shiny. The warp and weft are different colors, which creates a shimmering or iridescent surface. The hand is usually soft due to the fiber content.

7. Silk habotai is a fine woven ribbon that is similar to silk bias ribbon but has a finished selvage edge. The hand is soft.

8. Single-sided satin ribbon has one shiny side and one dull side. The hand is soft to medium, depending on the fiber content.

9. Taffeta ribbon has a fine, tight, even weave; often the warp and weft are different colors to create a changeable surface. The hand is soft to medium due to the fiber content.

10. Twill tape is a cotton tape with a subtle woven pattern. The hand is stiff due to the thickness of the fibers.

11. Velvet ribbon has a plush finish on one side and a flat finish on the other side. The hand is medium to stiff, depending on the fiber content.

Lace

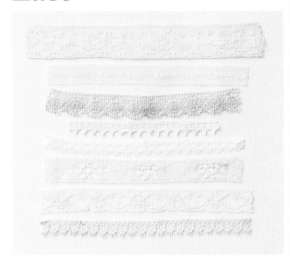

Variety of laces

Flat-edge lace comes in a variety of patterns, textures, and widths and is found in cotton or synthetic fibers. The hand is determined by the design and the fiber content. These laces can be used alone in some of the simpler ribbonwork techniques or combined with a ribbon to create a unique trim. The hand can be soft to stiff, depending on the fiber content and weave.

1. Gentle Lady; 2. Rosette; 3. Gala Gather Petal Flower; 4. Posy; 5. Star Point Petal Flower

Creating Unique Ribbon Trims

Variety of flowers made from unique ribbons

There are a few simple techniques you can use to create a unique trim. These can be used for any design that calls for a woven ribbon.

TWO-COLOR RIBBON

This trim can be used for any flower, leaf, or other design.

1. Select 2 lengths of ribbon, either the same width or different widths; line up the selvage edges.

2. Machine stitch the inner selvage edges together with a zigzag stitch. Follow the directions for the design using the new combined width.

FANCY-EDGE RIBBON

This trim can be used for any flower, leaf, or other design that has a gathered inner selvage edge.

1. Select 2 ribbons or 1 ribbon and 1 lace, the same width or different widths.

2. Machine or hand stitch the second ribbon or lace to the outer selvage edge of the first ribbon.

3. Follow the directions for the design using the new combined width.

INNER EDGE LAYERING

This trim can be used for any flower, leaf, or other design that has a gathered inner selvage edge.

1. Select 2 ribbons, 1 wide and 1 narrower.

2. Cut the wider ribbon according to the directions for the design. Pin the narrow ribbon along the bottom selvage edge of the wider width. Cut off the excess ribbon.

3. Follow the remaining directions for the design.

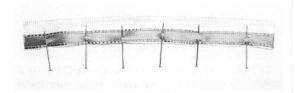

SHADOW LAYERING

This trim can be used for any flower, leaf, or other design that has a gathered inner or outer selvage edge or is gathered through the center width of the project ribbon.

1. Select a ribbon and a lace the same width.

2. Cut the ribbon according to the directions for the design. Pin the lace to the ribbon along the bottom selvage edge; cut off the excess lace.

3. Follow the remaining directions for the design.

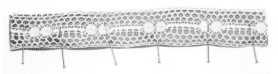

CENTER WIDTH LAYERING

This trim can be used for any flower, leaf, or other design that has a gathered inner or outer selvage edge or is gathered through the center width of the project ribbon.

1. Select 2 ribbons, 1 wider and 1 narrower.

2. Cut the wider ribbon according to the directions for the design. Pin the narrow ribbon through the center of the width of the wider ribbon; cut off the excess ribbon.

3. Machine or hand stitch the narrow ribbon to the wider ribbon.

4. Follow the remaining directions for the design.

RIBBONWORK TECHNIQUES
AND CONSTRUCTION BASICS

Mariposa Fall, 4½" × 5"

Choosing Your Materials

COLOR

When you are choosing a ribbon or group of ribbons for your project, the first thing you usually think about is color. I suggest starting with colors you like and that are realistic for your project. I suggest this even for when you are practicing the techniques.

If you are working with an ombré or variegated ribbon, the color may change through the width or through the length. Keep in mind that the gathered side will be the center of the flower, bud, or leaf.

Rosettes made from two different edges of variegated ribbon; Folded Petal Flower using both sides of ribbon

WIDTH OF RIBBON

Another thing to keep in mind is the width of the ribbon. This is a factor when making something to fit into a section of a crazy quilt, or when making a corsage or a pin for a hat. In most cases, the design is round, and the end result will be twice the original width of the ribbon.

Rosettes and Rosettes with inner edge layering worked in a variety of widths and types of ribbon

RIBBON PROPERTIES

Each type of ribbon has special characteristics that make it perfect for one technique but not ideal for another. A good rule of thumb is to keep the technique simple for a one-sided woven or printed ribbon; a more elaborate technique can look fabulous using a basic staple such as an inexpensive satin ribbon.

1. Posy made from cotton twill tape; 2. Irish Rose made from satin ribbon; 3. Figure 8 Leaf used as bow with button

Construction Techniques

The techniques I have included in this book range from very simple to more complex, with corresponding levels of skill required. A technique may use a single length of ribbon or many individual lengths of ribbon. The ribbon may be marked, pinned, or folded and then sewn to form the specific designs. A technique may call for the width of the ribbon to be folded, thus adding the selvage or bias edges as an additional design detail.

The three main types of construction are tube length, flat length, and individual parts. The first two techniques finish off the raw edges of the design using different methods. Both hide the raw edges of the ribbon on the wrong side of the flower. The techniques used for individual parts all have raw edges that will be hidden in the construction process or when assembled with another component.

TUBE LENGTH

The raw edges of the ribbon are stitched together first to form a circle. The inside selvage edge of the ribbon is gathered to form the middle of the flower. Use a single- or double-sided ribbon with a soft to medium hand.

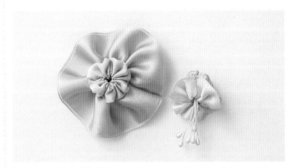

Rosette with Ruffled Rosette Center and Cup and Saucer Vine

FLAT LENGTH

The length of the ribbon is gathered to form the center of the flower. The raw edges are stitched directly parallel to the cut edge or angled away from the cut edge, forming two curved edges that fold in to meet the center of the flower. A variation may include one edge beginning with a knot. Use a single- or double-sided ribbon with a soft to medium hand.

Knotted Posy and Cockle Shell

Variations of flat length construction include folding or stitching to create individual petals or parts with one length of ribbon.

Boat Gather Petals

The individual petals are marked and then gather stitched with a straight edge on either side of the length of the petal and straight across the bottom selvage edge. This technique can be worked for one length of ribbon, or the ribbon can be cut into lengths to create individual petals. Use a single- or double-sided ribbon with a soft to medium hand.

Pansy and Boat Gather Petal Flower with Single Knot

Crinkle Fold Petals

This technique can be used for a short or long length of petals. The ribbon is folded back and forth at a 90° angle for each petal. There are a variety of ways to stitch the folds that create different shaped petals. Both the outer and inner edges are folded; the gathers form a highly textured surface. Use a double-sided ribbon with a soft to medium hand.

Crinkle Fold Petal Flower and Snail

Flip 'n Fold Petals

An angled fold forms the first petal; the following petals are folded one revolution behind or in front of the previous petal. Each petal is pinned or stitched in place before the next petal is formed. When gathered, the petals form a unique round curve with a pretty center. Use a double-sided ribbon with a soft to stiff hand.

Symphony Rose and Flip 'n Fold Petal Flower

Folded Petals

The first petal is measured to length, and then the ribbon is folded at a 90° angle to begin the next petal. The length of the petals can be the same or varied within the design. The entire length of ribbon is gathered, creating full, round petals. Use a double-sided ribbon with a soft to medium hand.

Windflower and Nemesia

Gala Gather Petals

The individual petals are marked and then stitched with a straight edge on either side of the length of the petal. The bottom and top selvage edges are stitched oppositely, with the finished stitching resembling a serpentine pattern. This creates soft curved petals that are formed both on the outer edge and inner edge. Use a single- or double-sided ribbon with a soft to medium hand.

Claire de Lune and Gala Gather Petal Flower

Gather and Grab Petals

The individual petals are marked and then each petal is stitched along the bottom selvage edge, with the first and last petals with straight side edges. The inner petals have side edges that are merely caught by one short running stitch at the top selvage edge. This technique is particularly suited for a double-edge silk bias ribbon or two layers of woven ribbon.

Hibiscus and Gather and Grab Petal Flower

Gathered Loop Petals

The individual petals are marked and then the first and last petals are gather stitched with straight side edges; the lengths of the inner petals are folded and then stitched across the fold. When pulled tightly, the length forms individual petals with soft curves. Use a double-sided ribbon with a soft to medium hand.

Gathered Loop Petal Flower and Moulin Rouge

Hop 'n Stitch Petals

The length of ribbon is marked down the center width for each petal; each mark is then stitched with one short running stitch. When pulled tightly, the length forms individual square-tipped petals, with a detailed center. Use a double-sided ribbon with a soft to stiff hand.

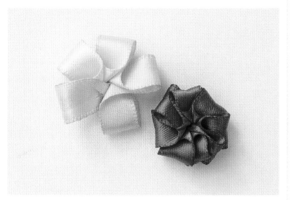

Hop 'n Stitch Petals: 5 3RW petal flower and 8 2RW petal flower

Ruched Petals

The individual petals are marked and then stitched with an angled edge on either side of the length of the petal. When the ribbon is gathered, softly curving petals with slightly pointed tips are formed on either side of the width of the ribbon. Use a single- or double-sided ribbon with a soft to stiff hand.

Queen's Climber and Ruched Petal Flower

Pouf Gathers

This is a simple and fast technique using one length of ribbon to create a row of pleasing but irregular petals that can be used for either a flower or center. Use a single- or double-sided ribbon with a soft to stiff hand.

Pouf Gather Center and Pennine Mum

Star Point Petals

The individual petals are marked and then stitched with a straight edge on either side of the length of the petal. This creates unique pointed-tip petals with unstitched inner edges. Use a single- or double-sided ribbon with a soft to medium hand.

Star Point Petal Flower and Pretty Lady with ribbon detail

UNIQUE CONSTRUCTION TECHNIQUES

A few of the techniques in the book simply defy specific construction terms. These techniques for the most part have individual free-form folds that are stitched and sculpted to create the petals.

Chou Rose and Vintage Favorite

INDIVIDUAL PARTS

Petals and Leaves

These individually cut parts are made using a variety of techniques in which the ribbon is measured and cut into specific lengths. For a flower, these pieces will be stitched together with the raw edges hidden under the center of the flower, or they will be assembled to a base with a separate stitched center hiding the raw edges. The raw edges of a leaf will be hidden under a flower.

1. Columbine (Boat Gather Petals and Calla Lily Petals);
2. Estrella (Bandana Fold Petals); 3. Heliotrope (Pinch Tip Petals)

Centers

Some of these techniques are similar to the flower construction techniques, and some are not. The centers may also include stamens, which can be purchased from specialty stores. Some flowers will have a French knot stitched with silk embroidery ribbon. A special button can also be used for a center.

Group of flowers with different center details

BEGINNING FLOWERS

*The flowers and leaves in this chapter represent the basic techniques
included in this book. Use these techniques as a stepping-off point
for the designs in the chapters that follow.*

ROSETTE ... 25
⅜" satin ribbon with
Prairie Point Leaf:
⅝" satin ribbon

HOP 'N STITCH PETALS ... 32
⅜" satin ribbon with
Miter Fold Leaf:
⅜" satin ribbon

POSY ... 26
⅝" and ⅜" satin ribbon with
Tuxedo Fold Leaf:
⅝" satin ribbon

STAR POINT PETALS ... 33
⅜" satin ribbon with
Slender Tip Leaf-M:
⅜" satin ribbon

KNOTTED POSY ... 27
½" satin ribbon and
Knotted Ruffled Posy:
⅜" satin ribbon

FOLDED PETALS ... 34
½" satin ribbon with
Loop Leaf-M:
½" woven ribbon

DOUBLE POSY AND FANCY ROSETTE OR POSY ... 28
½" and ⅜" satin ribbon and
Double Posy: ⅜" satin ribbon

GATHERED LOOP PETALS ... 35
⅜" satin ribbon with
Box Fold Leaf-M:
⅜" satin ribbon

BOAT GATHER PETALS ... 29
⅝" satin ribbon with
Pinch Tip Leaf-M:
⅝" French wire ribbon

RUCHED PETALS ... 36
⅜" satin ribbon with
Neapolitan Leaf-M:
⅜" satin ribbon

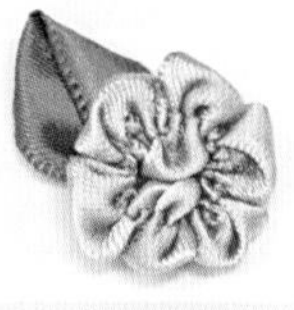

GATHER AND GRAB PETALS ... 30
1" silk bias ribbon with
Bandana Fold Leaf:
1½" silk bias ribbon

CRINKLE FOLD PETALS ... 37
½" satin ribbon with
Soft Curve Leaf:
½" satin ribbon

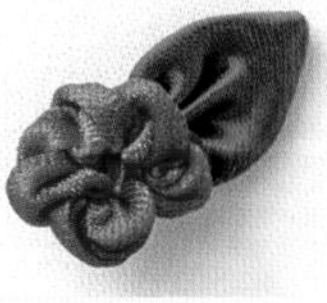

GALA GATHER PETALS ... 31
⅜" satin ribbon with
Rooftop Leaf-M:
⅜" satin ribbon

FLIP 'N FOLD PETALS ... 38
⅜" satin ribbon with
Simple Leaf:
⅝" satin ribbon

Rosette

Rosette with Prairie Point Leaf (page 111). Use ribbon ¼" wider for leaf than for flower.

SKILL LEVEL: *Easy* ◆

Suggested Ribbon

Woven or French wire ribbon with a soft, medium, or stiff hand, single- or double-sided

Amount Needed

▪ **Soft-hand ribbon:**

8 × width of project ribbon

▪ **Medium-hand ribbon:**

9 × width of project ribbon

▪ **Stiff-hand ribbon:**

10 × width of project ribbon

DIRECTIONS

See General Directions (page 144).

1. Cut 1 length of ribbon (see chart) according to the hand of the project ribbon. Fold the ribbon length in half, right side in, matching the raw edges. Stitch the raw edges together with a ⅛" seam allowance using assembly stitch 2. Anchor knot the thread into the selvage edges.

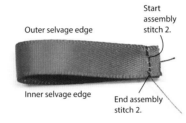

Outer selvage edge

Start assembly stitch 2.

Inner selvage edge

End assembly stitch 2.

2. Starting at the inner selvage edge next to the seam, gather stitch along the continuous selvage edge back to the seam (through only 1 layer of ribbon).

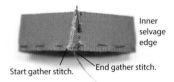

Inner selvage edge

Start gather stitch.   End gather stitch.

3. Gently pull the thread tight to form the middle of the flower. Tackstitch and anchor knot the thread.

Tackstitch.

Finished flower. Detail option: French knot (page 133)

Measure and Cut

Ribbon width (RW)	Soft-hand: Cut 1 length 8RW.	Medium-hand: Cut 1 length 9RW.	Stiff-hand: Cut 1 length 10RW.
1"	8"	9"	10"
⅞"	7"	7⅞"	8¾"
¾"	6"	6¾"	7½"
⅝"	5"	5⅝"	6¼"
½"	4"	4½"	5"
⅜"	3"	3⅜"	3¾"
¼"	2"	2¼"	2½"

Posy

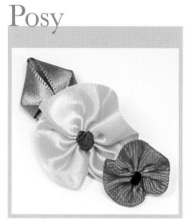

Posy with Tuxedo Fold Leaf (page 122). Use same ribbon width for both flower and leaf.

SKILL LEVEL: **Easy** ◆

Suggested Ribbon

Woven or French wire ribbon with a soft, medium, or stiff hand, single- or double-sided

Amount Needed

■ **Soft-hand ribbon:** 8 × width of project ribbon

■ **Medium-hand ribbon:** 9 × width of project ribbon

■ **Stiff-hand ribbon:** 10 × width of project ribbon

DIRECTIONS

See General Directions (page 144).

1. Cut 1 length of ribbon (see chart) according to the hand of the project ribbon. Mark 1RW from each raw edge. Anchor knot the thread into the outer selvage edge, ⅛″ from the raw edge. Gather stitch at an angle to the mark at the inner selvage edge.

2. Loop over the edge and continue gather stitching along the selvage edge to the remaining mark; loop over the edge. Gather stitch at an angle to the outer selvage edge, ⅛″ from the raw edge.

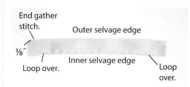

3. Stitch through the selvage edge next to the beginning anchor knot. Gently pull the thread to form the middle of the flower.

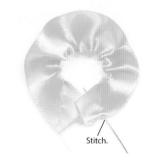

4. Match the right sides of the raw edges. Pull the thread tight. Tackstitch and anchor knot the thread.

Finished flower. Detail option: French knot (page 133)

Measure and Cut

Ribbon width (RW)	Soft-hand: Cut 1 length 8RW.	Medium-hand: Cut 1 length 9RW.	Stiff-hand: Cut 1 length 10RW.
1″	8″	9″	10″
⅞″	7″	7⅞″	8¾″
¾″	6″	6¾″	7½″
⅝″	5″	5⅝″	6¼″
½″	4″	4½″	5″
⅜″	3″	3⅜″	3¾″
¼″	2″	2¼″	2½″

Knotted Posy and Knotted Ruffled Posy

Knotted Posy and Knotted Ruffled Posy

SKILL LEVEL: **Easy** ◆

Suggested Ribbon

Woven or French wire ribbon with a soft, medium, or stiff hand, double-sided

Amount Needed

- 13 × width of project ribbon plus ½"

Measure and Cut

Ribbon width (RW)	Cut 1 length 13RW plus ½".
1"	13½"
⅞"	11⅞"
¾"	10¼"
⅝"	8⅝"
½"	7"
⅜"	5⅜"

DIRECTIONS

See General Directions (page 144) and Posy (page 26).

Knotted Posy

1. Cut 1 length of ribbon 13RW plus ½" (see chart). Tie an overhand knot close to the raw edge; leave a ½" tail below the knot. Mark 1RW from the remaining raw edge. Anchor knot the thread into the inner selvage edge at the knot. Follow Posy, Step 2 (page 26).

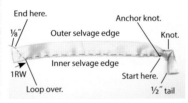

2. From the wrong side, stitch through the selvage edge next to the beginning anchor knot. Gently pull the thread to form the middle of the flower. Position the knot in the center of the flower.

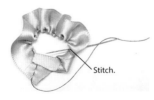

3. Pull the thread tight. Stitch back through the center to the wrong side. Tackstitch and anchor knot the thread.

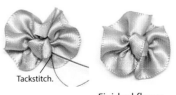

Finished flower

Knotted Ruffled Posy

1. Cut 1 length of ribbon 13RW plus ½" (see chart). Follow the knot directions in Step 1 at left. Fold the width of ribbon in half and mark ½RW from the opposite raw edge. Anchor knot the thread into the inner selvage edges at the knot. Follow Posy, Step 2 (page 26), stitching through both layers of ribbon.

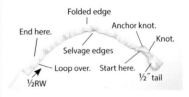

2. Follow Steps 2 and 3 for the Knotted Posy.

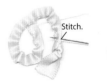

Finished flower

Double Posy and Fancy Rosette or Posy

Fancy Rosettes and Posies and Double Posy

SKILL LEVEL: **Easy** ◆

Suggested Ribbon

Woven or French wire ribbon with a soft or medium hand, single- or double-sided, or substitute a piece of lace for the narrower width of ribbon for the Fancy Rosette or Posy

Amount Needed

- **Double Posy:** 12 × width of project ribbon

- **Fancy Rosette or Posy:** 12 × width of wider ribbon and a narrower ribbon or piece of lace in same width

 tip

The center of this flower is usually very large; it can be covered with a button, French knot (page 133), or Single Knot (page 128).

Measure and Cut

Ribbon width (RW)	Cut each length 12RW.
1"	12"
⅞"	10½"
¾"	9"
⅝"	7½"
½"	6"
⅜"	4½"

DIRECTIONS

Double Posy

See General Directions (page 144) and Knotted Posy (page 27).

1. Cut 1 length 12RW (see chart). Fold the length of ribbon in half. Mark 1RW from the raw edges. Anchor knot the thread into the outer selvage edges ⅛" in from the raw edges. Gather stitch at an angle to the mark at the inner selvage edges, stitching through both layers of ribbon. Loop over the edge and gather stitch along the selvage edges through both layers of ribbon to the fold.

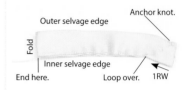

2. Follow Step 2 for the Knotted Posy, with the beginning curve in the center.

3. Follow Step 3 for the Knotted Posy.

Finished flower

Fancy Rosette or Posy

See General Directions (page 144), Creating Unique Ribbon Trims (page 15), and Rosette (page 25) or Posy (page 26).

Cut 1 length of ribbon 12RW (see chart) from the widest ribbon. Follow the directions for inner edge layering, shadow layering, or center width layering using the narrower ribbon or lace. Follow the assembly directions for the Rosette or Posy.

1. Rosette and Posy with inner edge layering; 2. Rosette and Posy with shadow layering; 3. Rosette and Posy with center width layering

Boat Gather Petals

Boat Gather Petal Flower with Pinch Tip Leaf-M (page 113). Use same ribbon width for both flower and leaf.

SKILL LEVEL: **Easy** ◆

Suggested Ribbon

Woven or French wire ribbon with a soft or medium hand, single- or double-sided

Amount Needed

▪ Approximately 9 × width of project ribbon plus ½"*

Measure

Ribbon width (RW)	Measure 3RW per petal.*
1"	3"
⅞"	2⅝"
¾"	2¼"
⅝"	1⅞"
½"	1½"
⅜"	1⅛"

* Do not cut the ribbon until instructed to do so.

DIRECTIONS

See General Directions (page 144).

1. Mark ¼" from the raw edge. Measure and mark 3RW (see chart); this is the length of 1 petal. Measure and mark the next 2 petals from the previous mark. Cut the ribbon ¼" from the last mark.

2. Anchor knot the thread into the outer selvage edge at the first mark. Gather stitch to the inner selvage edge; loop over the edge. Continue stitching along the selvage edge, stopping just before the next mark; loop over the edge. Gather stitch up to the outer selvage edge. This completes 1 petal.

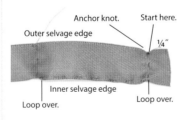

3. Gather stitch to the inner selvage edge, mirroring the stitches (page 143) in the previous row, and loop over the edge. Repeat for the next petal; gather stitch to the outer selvage edge at the last mark to finish the last petal.

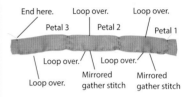

4. Stitch through the selvage edge next to the beginning anchor knot. Gently pull the thread to form the petals and middle of the flower. Match the right sides of the raw edges. Pull the thread tight. Tackstitch and anchor knot into the raw edges.

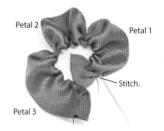

Finished flower. Detail option: French knot (page 133)

Gather and Grab Petals

Gather and Grab Petal Flower with Bandana Fold Leaf (page 114). Use ribbon ½" wider for leaf than for flower.

SKILL LEVEL: **Easy** ◆

Suggested Ribbon

Silk bias or woven habotai ribbon

Amount Needed

- Approximately 12 × width of project ribbon plus ½"*

Measure

Ribbon width (RW)	Measure 3RW per petal.*
1"	3"
¾"	2¼"
⅝"	1⅞"
½"	1½"
⁷⁄₁₆"	1⁵⁄₁₆"

* Do not cut the ribbon until instructed to do so.

 note

Use the original width of the ribbon to calculate the RW measurements.

DIRECTIONS

See General Directions (page 144).

1. Fold and gently finger-press the width of the ribbon to ⅝ the original width. Insert a pin ¼" from the raw edge. Measure 3RW (see chart) and insert a pin; this is the length of 1 petal. Pin the remaining 3 petals from the last pin of the previous petal. Cut the ribbon ¼" from the last pin.

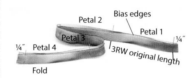

2. Anchor knot the thread into the outer bias edge at the pin. Gather stitch to the inner folded edge; loop over the edge. Continue stitching along the folded edge to the next pin.

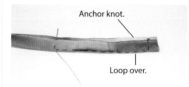

3. From behind, take a stitch through both layers of ribbon to the outer bias edge. This completes 1 petal.

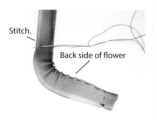

4. Slightly pull the thread to form the petal. Repeat the stitching in Steps 2 and 3 for 2 more petals. Gather stitch to the outer bias edge at the last pin to finish the last petal.

5. Stitch through the selvage edge next to the beginning anchor knot. Match the right sides of the raw edges. Gently pull the thread to form the middle of the flower. Pull the thread tight. Tackstitch and anchor the thread.

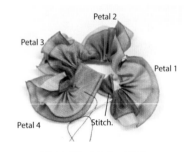

Finished flower. Detail option: French knot (page 133)

Gala Gather Petals

Gala Gather Petal Flower with Rooftop Leaf-M (page 114). Use same ribbon width for both flower and leaf.

SKILL LEVEL: **Easy** ◆

Suggested Ribbon

Woven or French wire ribbon with a soft or medium hand, double-sided

Amount Needed

- Approximately 27 × width of project ribbon plus ½"*

Measure

Ribbon width (RW)	Measure 3RW per petal.*
1"	3"
⅞"	2⅝"
¾"	2¼"
⅝"	1⅞"
½"	1½"
⅜"	1⅛"

Do not cut the ribbon until instructed to do so.

DIRECTIONS

See General Directions (page 144).

1. Mark ¼" from the raw edge. Measure and mark 3RW (see chart) from the mark; this is the length of 1 petal. Mark each of the remaining 8 petals from the previous mark, alternating selvage edges. Cut the ribbon ¼" from the last mark.

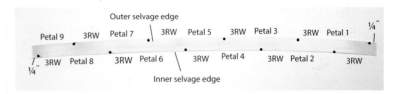

2. Anchor knot the thread into the outer selvage edge at the first mark. Gather stitch to the inner selvage edge; loop over the edge. Continue stitching along the selvage edge, stopping just before the next mark; loop over the edge. Gather stitch up to the outer selvage edge. This is 1 petal. Gather stitch along the outer edge to the next mark; loop over the edge. Gather stitch to the inner selvage edge. This is the next petal.

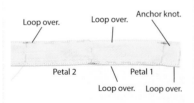

3. Repeat for each of the remaining 7 petals, following the stitch pattern in Step 2. Stitch through the selvage edge next to the beginning anchor knot. Gently pull the thread to form the petals and middle of the flower.

4. Match the right sides of the raw edges. Pull the thread tight, allowing the inner petals to touch. Tackstitch and anchor knot into the raw edges.

Finished flower

Hop 'n Stitch Petals

Hop 'n Stitch Petal Flower with Miter Fold Leaf (page 115). Use same ribbon width for both flower and leaf.

SKILL LEVEL: *Easy* ◆

Suggested Ribbon

Woven or French wire ribbon with a soft or medium hand, double-sided

Amount Needed

■ Approximately 16 × width of project ribbon plus ½"*

Measure

Ribbon width (RW)	Measure 2RW per petal.*
1"	2"
⅞"	1¾"
¾"	1½"
⅝"	1¼"
½"	1"
⅜"	¾"
¼"	½"

* Do not cut the ribbon until instructed to do so.

DIRECTIONS

See General Directions (page 144).

1. Mark in the center of the width of ribbon ¼" from the raw edge. Measure and mark 2RW (see chart) from the previous mark; this is the length of 1 petal. Mark the remaining 7 petals from the mark of the previous petal. Cut the ribbon ¼" from the last mark.

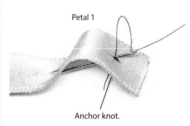

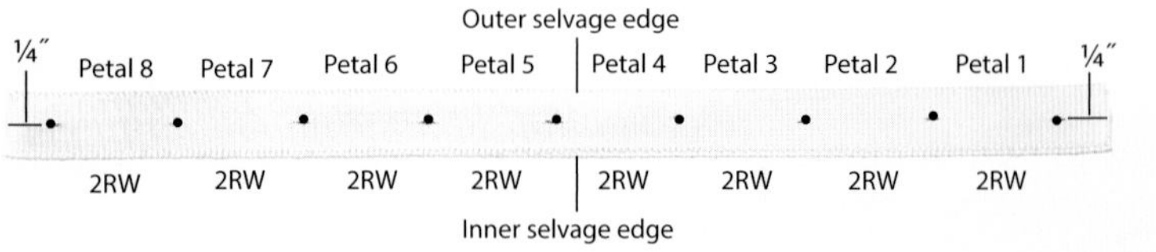

Outer selvage edge

¼" | Petal 8 | Petal 7 | Petal 6 | Petal 5 | Petal 4 | Petal 3 | Petal 2 | Petal 1 | ¼"

2RW 2RW 2RW 2RW 2RW 2RW 2RW 2RW

Inner selvage edge

2. Anchor knot the thread at the first mark in the center of the ribbon width. From behind, stitch a short stitch through the next mark; this completes 1 petal.

Repeat for the remaining petals, keeping the loops of ribbon on the needle.

Petal 1

Anchor knot.

3. Gently pull the thread through the middle of the flower. Overlap the raw edge of the first petal over the raw edge of the last petal. Stitch the needle through the ribbon above the mark on the first petal.

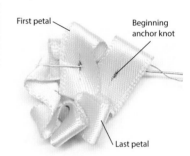

First petal

Beginning anchor knot

Last petal

4. Thread the needle back through the opening in the middle. Hold onto the raw edges; pull the thread tight. Tackstitch and anchor knot into the raw edges.

Tackstitch.

Finished flower

Star Point Petals

Star Point Petal Flower with Slender Tip Leaf-M (page 115). Use same ribbon width for both flower and leaf.

SKILL LEVEL: *Easy* ◆

Suggested Ribbon

Woven or French wire ribbon with a soft, medium, or stiff hand, single- or double-sided

Amount Needed

- Approximately 20 × width of project ribbon plus ½"*

Measure

Ribbon width (RW)	Measure 4RW per petal.*
1"	4"
⅞"	3½"
¾"	3"
⅝"	2½"
½"	2"
⅜"	1½"
¼"	1"

Do not cut the ribbon until instructed to do so.

DIRECTIONS

See General Directions (page 144).

1. Mark ¼" from the raw edge. Measure and mark 4RW (see chart) from the previous mark; this is the length of 1 petal. Mark the remaining 4 petals from the mark of the previous petal. Cut the ribbon ¼" from the last mark. Anchor knot the thread at the first mark on the outer selvage edge. Gather stitch to the inner selvage edge.

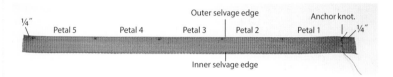

2. Skip to just before the next mark and gather stitch to the outer selvage edge; this completes 1 petal. Gather stitch to the inner selvage edge, mirroring the gather stitches (page 143) in the previous row. Pull the thread slightly to form the petal.

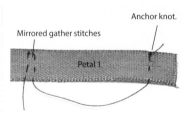

3. Repeat Step 2 for the next 3 petals; gather stitch to the outer selvage edge at the last mark to finish the last petal. Stitch through the selvage edge next to the beginning anchor knot. Gently

pull the thread tightly to form the middle of the flower.

4. Match the right sides of the raw edges together. Pull the thread tight. Tackstitch and anchor knot into the raw edges.

Finished flower. Detail option: French knot (page 133)

Folded Petals

Folded Petal Flower with Loop Leaf-M (page 112). Use same ribbon width for both flower and leaf.

SKILL LEVEL: *Easy* ◆

Suggested Ribbon

Woven or French wire ribbon with a soft or medium hand, double-sided

Amount Needed

■ Approximately 14 × width of project ribbon plus ½"*

Measure

Ribbon width (RW)	Measure 2RW per petal.*
1"	2"
⅞"	1¾"
¾"	1½"
⅝"	1¼"
½"	1"
⅜"	¾"
¼"	½"

* Do not cut the ribbon until instructed to do so.

DIRECTIONS

See General Directions (page 144).

1. Mark ¼" in from the raw edge with a pin. Measure 2RW (see chart), fold the ribbon down at a 90° angle, and insert a pin through the fold.

Begin measuring here for next petal.

← 2RW → | ¼"

2. Measure and fold 2RW from the previous fold; fold the ribbon in the same direction. Repeat for 2 more petals. Measure and pin 2RW from the last mark. Cut the ribbon ¼" beyond the last pin.

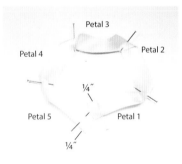

Petal 3
Petal 4
Petal 2
¼"
Petal 5
Petal 1
¼"

3. Anchor knot the thread at the ¼" mark on the outer selvage edge. Gather stitch to the inner selvage edge; loop over the edge. Continue along each selvage edge and through each fold to the last mark; loop over each edge. Gather stitch to the outer selvage edge. Stitch through the selvage edge next to the beginning anchor knot.

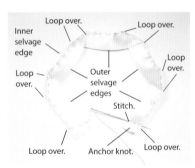

Loop over. Loop over.
Inner selvage edge
Loop over.
Loop over. Outer selvage edges
Stitch.
Loop over. Anchor knot. Loop over.

4. Gently pull the thread to form the middle of the flower. Match the right sides of the raw edges. Pull the thread tight. Tackstitch and anchor knot into the raw edges.

Tackstitch.

Finished flower. Detail option: French knot (page 133)

Gathered Loop Petals

Gathered Loop Petal Flower with Box Fold Leaf-M (page 113). Use same ribbon width for both flower and leaf.

SKILL LEVEL: *Intermediate* ◆◆

Suggested Ribbon

Woven or French wire ribbon with a soft or medium hand, double-sided

Amount Needed

■ Approximately 18 × width of project ribbon plus ½"*

Measure

Ribbon width (RW)	Measure 3RW per petal.*
1"	3"
⅞"	2⅝"
¾"	2¼"
⅝"	1⅞"
½"	1½"
⅜"	1⅛"

* Do not cut the ribbon until instructed to do so.

DIRECTIONS

See General Directions (page 144).

1. Pin ¼" from the raw edge. Measure and pin 3RW (see chart) from the previous pin; this is the length of 1 petal. Pin each of the remaining 5 petals from the last pin of the previous petal. Cut the ribbon ¼" from the last pin. Anchor knot the thread at the first pin on the selvage edge.

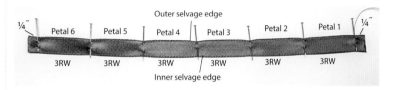

2. Gather stitch across the width of the ribbon, beginning with the needle on the top side of the ribbon and ending with the needle on the underside of the ribbon.

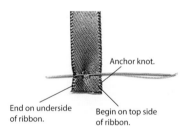

Anchor knot.
End on underside of ribbon.
Begin on top side of ribbon.

3. Fold the length of ribbon at the next pin, right sides together. Gather stitch through the fold through both layers of ribbon across the width of the ribbon, as in Step 2. Repeat for the remaining 4 petals.

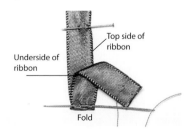

Underside of ribbon
Top side of ribbon
Fold

4. Fold the length of the ribbon down at the last pin and gather stitch across the width of the ribbon as in Step 2. Stitch through the selvage edge next to the beginning anchor knot. Gently pull the thread to form the middle of the flower; allow each petal to overlap the previous petal.

6 5 4 3 2 Petal 1
Stitch.

5. Match the right sides of the raw edges together. Pull the thread tight; stitch back through the middle to the wrong side. Tackstitch and anchor knot into the raw edges.

Tackstitch.

Finished flower. Detail option: French knot (page 133)

Ruched Petals

Ruched Petal Flower with Neapolitan Leaf-M (page 118). Use same ribbon width for both flower and leaf.

SKILL LEVEL: **Intermediate** ◆◆

Suggested Ribbon

Woven or French wire ribbon with a soft or medium hand, single- or double-sided

Amount Needed

▪ Approximately 15 × width of project ribbon plus ½"*

Measure

Ribbon width (RW)	Measure 3RW per petal.*
1"	3"
⅞"	2⅝"
¾"	2¼"
⅝"	1⅞"
½"	1½"
⅜"	1⅛"

* Do not cut the ribbon until instructed to do so.

DIRECTIONS

See General Directions (page 144).

1. Mark ¼" from the raw edge. Measure and mark 3RW (see chart) from the previous mark; this is the length of 1 petal. Mark each of the remaining 4 petals from the mark of the previous petal. Cut the ribbon ¼" from the last mark. Anchor knot the thread at the first mark on the outer selvage edge.

The selvage edge facing away from you as you stitch is the outer edge of the flower. Petals are also formed along the inner edge, with 1 fewer lobe than the outer edge.

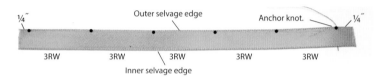

2. Fold the length of the ribbon halfway between the first and second marks to make a crease.

3. Gather stitch at an angle toward the crease at the inner selvage edge; loop over the edge. Gather stitch at an angle to the next mark at the outer selvage edge; loop over the edge. This completes 1 petal. Repeat Steps 2 and 3 for each of the remaining 4 petals.

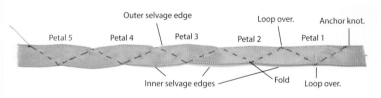

4. Stitch through the selvage edge next to the beginning anchor knot. Gently pull the thread to form the middle of the flower.

5. Match the right sides of the raw edges. Allow the inner petals to rise up slightly. Pull the thread tight. Tackstitch and anchor knot into the raw edges.

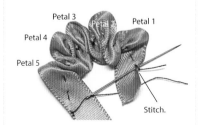

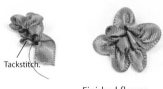

Finished flower

Crinkle Fold Petals

Crinkle Fold Petal Flower with Soft Curve Leaf (page 111). Use same ribbon width for both flower and leaf.

SKILL LEVEL: *Intermediate* ◆◆

Suggested Ribbon

Woven or French wire ribbon with a soft, medium, or stiff hand, double-sided

Amount Needed

▪ Approximately 12 × width of project ribbon plus ½"*

Measure

Ribbon width (RW)	Measure 1RW per petal.*
1"	1"
⅞"	⅞"
¾"	¾"
⅝"	⅝"
½"	½"
⅜"	⅜"

* Do not cut the ribbon until instructed to do so.

DIRECTIONS

See General Directions (page 144).

1. Measure ¼" from the raw edge. Fold the ribbon over and to the left at a 90° angle; pin through the fold.

Fold the ribbon over and up at an angle as shown; pin through the fold.

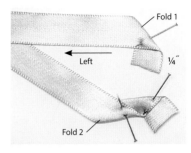

2. Repeat the fold directions in Step 1 for 10 more petals. Measure ¼" from the last folded edge; cut off the excess ribbon.

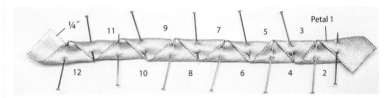

3. Anchor knot the thread at the beginning of the first fold. Gather stitch through both layers of ribbon along the selvage edge; loop over the edge. Repeat for the remaining selvage edges and the last visible edge.

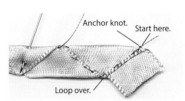

4. Stitch through the selvage edge next to the beginning anchor knot. Gently pull the thread to form the middle of the flower.

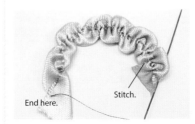

5. Match the right sides of the raw edges. Allow the inner petals to lie flat in the middle of the flower. Pull the thread tight. Tackstitch and anchor knot into the raw edges.

Finished flower

Flip 'n Fold Petals

Flip 'n Fold Petal Flower with Simple Leaf (page 112). Use ribbon ¼" wider for leaf than for flower.

Suggested Ribbon

Woven or French wire ribbon with a soft or medium hand, double-sided

Amount Needed

■ Approximately 7 × width of project ribbon plus ½"*

Measure

Ribbon width (RW)	Measure 1RW per petal.*
1"	1"
⅞"	⅞"
¾"	¾"
⅝"	⅝"
½"	½"
⅜"	⅜"

Do not cut the ribbon until instructed to do so.

DIRECTIONS

See General Directions (page 144).

1. Mark ¼" in from the raw edge. On the opposite selvage edge, mark 1RW (see chart). Anchor knot the thread at the first mark. Gather stitch at an angle toward the second mark.

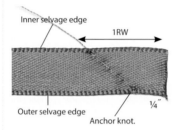

2. Fold the ribbon behind and down at a 90° angle and gather stitch across the fold through both layers of ribbon; loop over the edge. This completes the first petal.

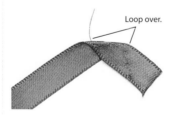

3. Repeat Step 2 for 4 more petals. Measure 1RW plus ¼" from the last fold; cut the ribbon. Gather stitch at an angle to the outer selvage edge, ¼" from the raw edge. This completes the last petal, for a total of 6 petals.

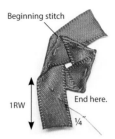

4. Gently pull the thread to form the petals and the middle of the flower. From behind, stitch through the selvage edge next to the beginning anchor knot.

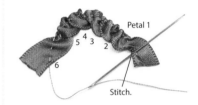

5. Holding onto the raw edges, with right sides together, pull the thread tight. Tackstitch and anchor knot into the raw edges.

Finished flower

VINTAGE FLOWERS

Imagine a garden full of flowering blossoms, lined up along a fence or clustered around a favorite tree. These flowers reflect the beauty of days gone by and remind us that time in the garden is time well spent.

note

The flowers listed in the following chart are accompanied by suggested leaf designs. In some cases, a leaf design is followed by a letter indicating leaf size.

S = Short   **M** = Medium   **L** = Long

For instructions to make the leaves, see Petals, Leaves, and Greenery (page 109).

ROSIE MANTLE ... 41
⅜" satin ribbon with
Ivy Leaf:
⅜" satin ribbon

CYMBIDIUM ... 47
⅜" and ½" satin ribbon with
Slender Tip Leaf-L:
⅜" satin ribbon

GAZANIA ... 42
⅜" satin ribbon and ⅛"
novelty ribbon with
Notched Leaf-L:
⅝" satin ribbon

PRIMROSE ... 48
1" and ½" silk bias ribbon with
Renaissance Leaf-S:
1½" silk bias ribbon

CASSIOPE ... 43
⅜" and ½" satin ribbon with
Sweet Leaf-M:
⅜" satin ribbon

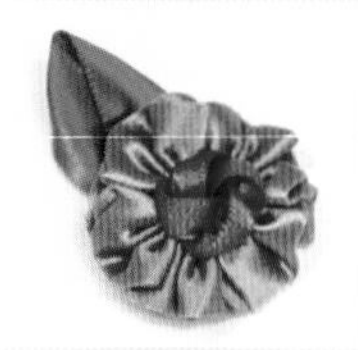

WINDFLOWER ... 49
⅝" silk satin ribbon and ⅝" satin
ribbon with *Deco Leaf-S:*
⅞" satin ribbon

SWEETHEART'S FLOWER ... 44
⅞" and ⅝" satin ribbon with
Soft Curve Leaf:
⅝" satin ribbon

PETUNIA ... 50
1" silk bias ribbon with
Art Nouveau Leaf-S:
1" French wire ribbon

CALLA LILY ... 45
1" silk satin ribbon with
Hooded Leaf-S:
1" French wire ribbon

PANSY ... 51
1" silk bias ribbon with
Oval Leaf-L:
1½" silk bias ribbon

HELIOTROPE ... 46
⅜" satin ribbon with
Art Nouveau Leaf-M:
⅜" satin ribbon

QUEEN'S CLIMBER ... 52
⅝" and ⅜" grosgrain ribbon
with *Baroque Leaf:*
⅞" novelty ribbon

Rosie Mantle

Rosie Mantle with Ivy Leaf (page 121). Use same ribbon width for both flower and leaf.

SKILL LEVEL: *Intermediate* ◆◆

Suggested Ribbon

Woven ribbon with a soft or medium hand, double-sided

Amount Needed

■ Approximately 39 × width of project ribbon plus ½"*

DIRECTIONS

See General Directions (page 144) and Hop 'n Stitch Petals (page 32).

1. Center petals: Cut 5 lengths of ribbon 3RW (see chart). Working with 1 piece, fold the length of ribbon in half; then fold the width of the ribbon in half. Tackstitch the raw edges together; do not cut the thread.

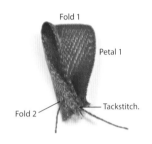

2. Fold a second length in half and anchor knot the thread ⅛" above the raw edges. Gather stitch across the width. Fold a third length and repeat, using the same thread.

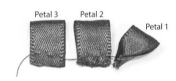

3. Arrange the second and third petals on each side of the first petal; pull in the gathers. Tackstitch, anchor knot, and cut the thread. Repeat Step 2 for the remaining 2 lengths, arranging these petals around the center on opposite sides of the first 2 petals. Anchor knot and cut the thread.

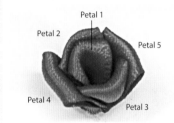

4. Outer petals: Mark 8 Hop 'n Stitch Petals 3RW (see chart). Follow the remaining directions for Hop 'n Stitch Petals through Step 3. Insert the center into the middle of the outer petals. Follow Step 4, arranging the petals evenly around the center.

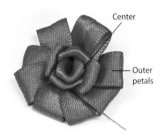

Finished flower

Measure and Cut

Ribbon width (RW)	Center petals	Outer petals
	Cut 5 lengths 3RW.	Measure 3RW per petal.*
1"	3"	3"
⅞"	2⅝"	2⅝"
¾"	2¼"	2¼"
⅝"	1⅞"	1⅞"
½"	1½"	1½"
⅜"	1⅛"	1⅛"

* Do not cut the ribbon until instructed to do so.

Gazania

Gazania with Notched Leaf-L (page 120). Use ribbon ¼″ wider for leaf than for petals.

Suggested Ribbon

3 different colors and 2 widths of woven ribbon with a soft or medium hand, double-sided

Amount Needed

■ **Petals**: approximately 72 × width of Color 1 ribbon plus ½″*

■ **Center**: 8 × width of Color 2 ribbon (Use same ribbon width as Color 1.)

■ **Petals and center**: approximately 80 × width of Color 3 ribbon (Use ribbon ¼″ narrower than Color 1.)

Additional Supplies

■ Silk embroidery ribbon

Measure and Cut

Ribbon width (RW)	Petals: Color 1	Center: Color 2
	Measure 6RW per petal.*	Cut 1 length 8RW.
1″	6″	8″
⅞″	5¼″	7″
¾″	4½″	6″
⅝″	3¾″	5″
½″	3″	4″
⅜″	2¼″	3″

* Do not cut the ribbon until instructed to do so.

DIRECTIONS

See General Directions (page 144), Center Width Layering (page 16), Star Point Petals (page 33), Inner Edge Layering (page 16), and Rosette (page 25).

1. Petals: Measure approximately 72RW of Color 1; follow the directions for center width layering using Color 3. Mark 12 Star Point Petals 6RW (see chart) and follow the remaining directions for Star Point Petals. Anchor knot and cut the thread.

2. Center: Cut 1 length of ribbon 8RW (see chart) from Color 2. Follow the directions for inner edge layering using Color 3. Follow the directions for the Rosette; do not cut the thread.

3. Flower: Tackstitch the center to the middle of the petals. Anchor knot the thread. Stitch a French knot (page 133) in the middle of the center.

Finished flower

Cassiope

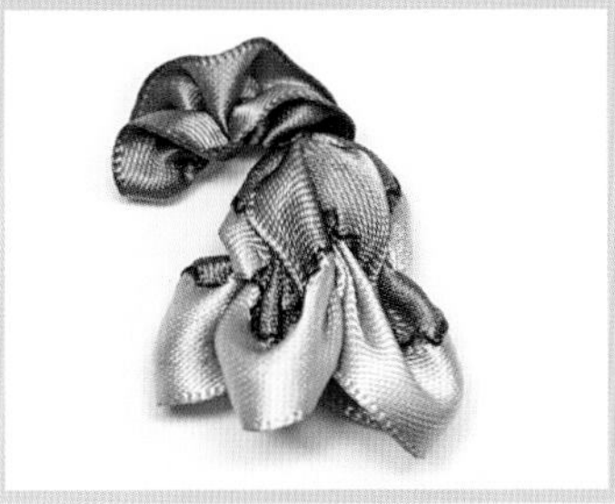

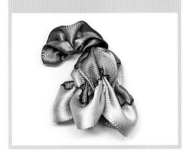

Cassiope with Sweet Leaf-M (page 117). Use same ribbon width for both calyx and leaf.

SKILL LEVEL: ***Intermediate***

Suggested Ribbon

2 different colors and widths of woven ribbon with a soft or medium hand, single- or double-sided

Amount Needed

- Approximately 8 × combined width of project ribbon plus 1″*

> **note**
>
> *Use 1 flower-colored ribbon with 1 leaf-colored ribbon ⅛″ narrower in the same length.*

Measure

Original ribbon width (RW)	Combined width	Measure 2RW per petal.*
¾″ and ⅝″	1⅜″	2¾″
⅝″ and ½″	1⅛″	2¼″
½″ and ⅜″	⅞″	1¾″
⅜″ and ¼″	⅝″	1¼″

** Do not cut the ribbon until instructed to do so.*

DIRECTIONS

See General Directions (page 144), Two-Color Ribbon (page 15), and Ruched Petals (page 36).

> **note**
>
> *Use the combined width to calculate the RW measurements.*

1. Using the wider width, measure approximately 8RW plus 1″ of both ribbons. Follow the directions for Two-Color Ribbon. Work with the flower color facing away from you. Mark 4 Ruched Petals 2RW (see chart) with a ½″ seam on both edges. Follow Ruched Petals through Step 3.

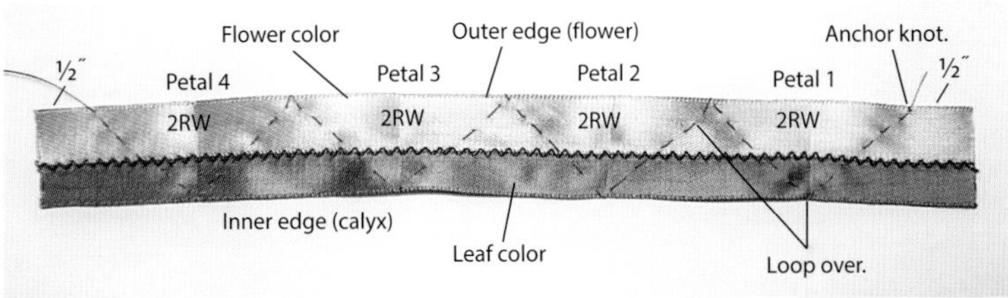

½″
Flower color
Petal 4
2RW
Outer edge (flower)
Petal 3
2RW
Petal 2
2RW
Anchor knot.
Petal 1
2RW
½″
Inner edge (calyx)
Leaf color
Loop over.

2. Follow Ruched Petals, Steps 4 and 5.

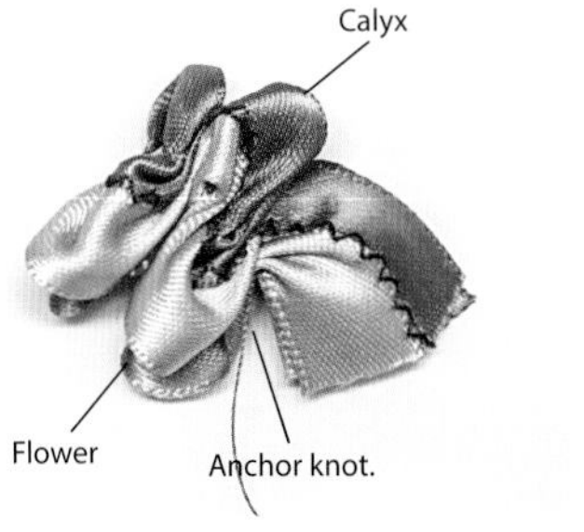

Calyx
Flower
Anchor knot.

3. Gather stitch ½″ from the raw edges; pull in the gathers. Tackstitch and anchor knot the thread. Trim the seam down to ¼″.

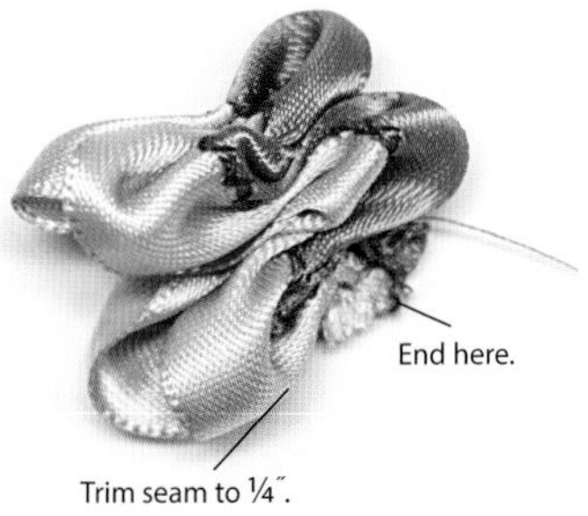

End here.
Trim seam to ¼″.

4. Whipstitch through each lobe of the calyx; pull in the stitches to close the top edge. Anchor knot the thread into the raw edges.

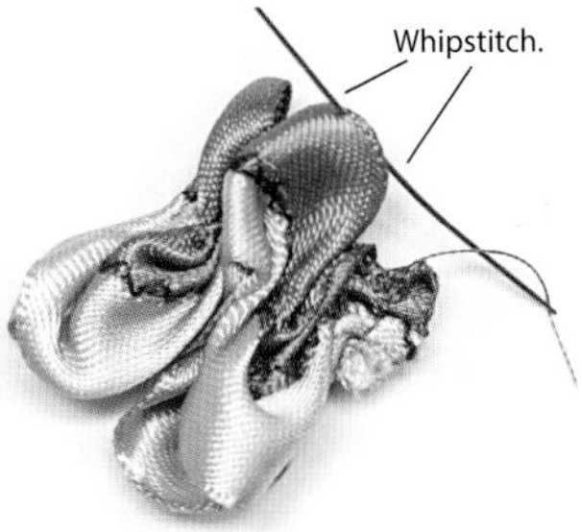

Whipstitch.

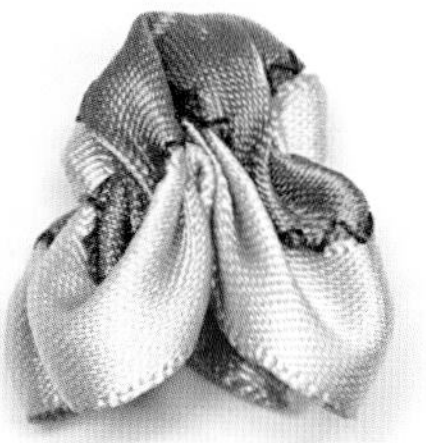

Finished flower

Sweetheart's Flower

Sweetheart's Flower with Soft Curve Leaf (page 111). Use same ribbon width for both center and leaf.

SKILL LEVEL: *Intermediate* ◆◆

Suggested Ribbon

2 different colors and widths of woven ribbon with a soft to medium hand, double-sided

Amount Needed

- **Outer layer:** 12 × width of Color 1 ribbon
- **Center:** Approximately 5 × width of Color 2 ribbon (Use ribbon ¼" narrower than Color 1.)*

Additional Supplies

- 1RW circle of crinoline

Measure and Cut

Ribbon width (RW)	Outer layer: Color 1	Center: Color 2
	Cut 1 length 12RW.	Measure 1RW per petal.*
1"	12"	1"
⅞"	10½"	⅞"
¾"	9"	¾"
⅝"	7½"	⅝"
½"	6"	½"

* Do not cut the ribbon until instructed to do so.

DIRECTIONS

See General Directions (page 144), Rosette (page 25), and Rose Bud Center (page 130).

1. Outer layer: Cut 1 length of ribbon 12RW (see chart). Follow Step 1 for the Rosette using assembly stitch 1. Fold the width of the ribbon in half. Follow Step 2, stitching through both layers of ribbon.

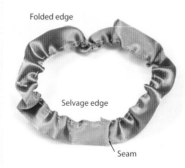

Folded edge

Selvage edge

Seam

2. Follow Step 3, leaving a ½RW opening in the middle of the flower. Tackstitch the gathered edges to the crinoline. Anchor knot and cut the thread.

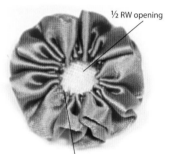

½ RW opening

Tackstitch gathered edges.

3. Center: Follow the directions for the Rose Bud Center; do not cut the thread.

4. Tuck the raw edges under and tackstitch into the middle of the crinoline. Anchor knot the thread.

Finished flower

Calla Lily

Calla Lily with Hooded Leaf-S (page 123). Use same ribbon width for both flower and leaf.

SKILL LEVEL: **Easy** ◆

Suggested Ribbon

Woven or French wire ribbon with a medium to stiff hand, double-sided

Amount Needed

■ 4 × width of project ribbon

Additional Supplies

■ 1 stamen

Measure and Cut

Ribbon width (RW)	Cut 1 length 4RW.
1"	4"
⅞"	3½"
¾"	3"
⅝"	2½"
½"	2"
⅜"	1½"

DIRECTIONS

See General Directions (page 144) and Prairie Point Leaf or Petal (page 111).

1. Cut 1 length of ribbon 4RW (see chart). Follow Step 1 for the Prairie Point Petal. Tackstitch the 2 halves of ribbon together at the selvage edge.

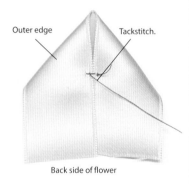

Outer edge   Tackstitch.

Back side of flower

2. Flip the ribbon over and place the stamen on top of the selvage edges; clip off the end of the stamen ¼" above the raw edges. Whipstitch the stamen and the selvage edges together.

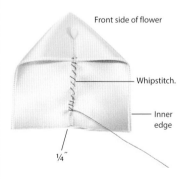

Front side of flower

Whipstitch.

Inner edge

¼"

3. Fold the left side in to the center, slightly beyond the stamen.

Tackstitch at the top edge of the fold.

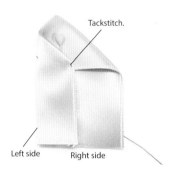

Tackstitch.

Left side   Right side

4. Repeat Step 3 for the right side, overlapping the left edge slightly. Fold the raw edges under ¼". Gather stitch across the folded edge, through all the layers of ribbon. Pull in the gathered stitches; tackstitch and anchor knot the thread.

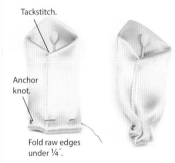

Tackstitch.

Anchor knot.

Fold raw edges under ¼".

Finished flower

Enchanted Lilies, 5½" × 6⅜"

Heliotrope

Heliotrope with Art Nouveau Leaf-M (page 119). Use same ribbon width for both flower and leaf.

SKILL LEVEL: *Intermediate* ◆◆

Suggested Ribbon

2 different colors of woven ribbon with a soft or medium hand, double-sided

Amount Needed

- **Center:** 10 × width of Color 1 ribbon
- **Petals:** 20 × width of Color 2 ribbon

DIRECTIONS

See General Directions (page 144), Single or Double Knot (page 128), Pinch Tip Leaf or Petal (page 113), and Simple Flower (page 116).

1. Center: Cut 1 length of ribbon 10RW (see chart). Follow the directions for the Double Knot.

Petals: Cut 5 lengths of ribbon 4RW (see chart). Follow the stitch, fold, and pin directions for the Pinch Tip Petal for each length.

2. Petals: Anchor knot the thread into the selvage edge of the first petal, ⅛" from the raw edge. Gather stitch across the width of the ribbon, beginning with the needle on the top side of the ribbon and ending with the needle on the underside of the ribbon.

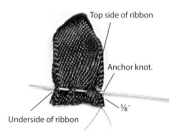

3. Repeat for each petal to join them together. Stitch through the top side of the selvage edge of the first petal, next to the beginning anchor knot.

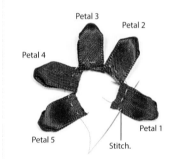

4. Follow Step 3 for the Simple Flower, inserting the center. Follow Step 4, allowing the petals to overlap slightly. Trim off the excess ribbon from the center.

Finished flower

Measure and Cut

Ribbon width (RW)	Center: Color 1	Petals: Color 2
	Cut 1 length 10RW.	Cut 5 lengths 4RW.
1"	10"	4"
⅞"	8¾"	3½"
¾"	7½"	3"
⅝"	6¼"	2½"
½"	5"	2"
⅜"	3¾"	1½"

Cymbidium

Cymbidium with Slender Tip Leaf-L (page 115). Use same ribbon width for both outer petals and leaf.

SKILL LEVEL: *Advanced* ◆◆◆

Suggested Ribbon

3 different colors and 2 widths of woven ribbon with a soft or medium hand, double-sided

Amount Needed

▪ **Inner petals:** 12 × width of Color 1 ribbon

▪ **Inner petals:** Color 2 ribbon (Use ribbon ⅛" narrower than Color 1 in same length.)

▪ **Outer petals:** 15 × width of Color 3 ribbon (Use ribbon ⅛" narrower than Color 1.)

Additional Supplies

▪ 5 folded stamens

Measure and Cut

Ribbon width (RW)	Inner petals: Colors 1 and 2	Ribbon width (RW)	Outer petals: Color 3
	Cut 3 lengths 4RW.		Cut 3 lengths 5RW.
1" and ⅞"	4"	⅞"	4⅜"
⅞" and ¾"	3½"	¾"	3¾"
¾" and ⅝"	3"	⅝"	3⅛"
⅝" and ½"	2½"	½"	2½"
½" and ⅜"	2"	⅜"	1⅞"

DIRECTIONS

See General Directions (page 144), Box Fold Leaf or Petal (page 113), Simple Flower (page 116), and Rooftop Leaf or Petal (page 114).

1. Cut 3 lengths of ribbon 4RW (see chart) from Color 1. Cut 3 lengths of ribbon from Color 2 the same length as Color 1; group these into pairs, with Color 2 on top. Follow the directions for the Box Fold Petal for each pair.

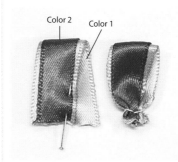

Color 2   Color 1

2. Follow Steps 2–4 for the Simple Flower, inserting the stamens through the center of the flower in Step 3. Anchor knot and cut the thread.

3. Cut 3 lengths of ribbon 5RW (see chart) from Color 3. Follow the fold and pin directions for the Rooftop Petal for each length. Repeat Step 2 above, inserting the inner petals into the outer petals.

Finished flower

Primrose

Primrose with Renaissance Leaf-S (page 117). Use ribbon ½″ wider for leaf than for petals.

SKILL LEVEL: *Easy* ◆

Suggested Ribbon

2 different colors and widths of silk bias ribbon: habotai or satin

Amount Needed

▪ **Center:** 2½ × width of Color 1 ribbon

▪ **Petals**: Approximately 7½ × width of Color 2 ribbon plus ½″* (Use ribbon ½″ wider than Color 1.)

Additional Supplies

▪ 1RW crinoline circle

Measure and Cut

Ribbon width (RW)	Center: Color 1	Ribbon width (RW)	Petals: Color 2
	Cut 1 length 2½RW.		Measure 1½RW per petal.*
1″	2½″	1½″	2¼″
½″	1¼″	1″	1½″

* Do not cut the ribbon until instructed to do so.

DIRECTIONS

See General Directions (page 144), Berry and Stuffed Berry (page 131), and Boat Gather Petals (page 29).

 note

Use the original width of the ribbon to calculate the RW measurements. Where the Boat Gather Petal directions refer to the outer selvage edge, that will be the folded edge in this flower; the inner selvage edge will be the bias edges in this flower.

1. Center: Cut 1 length of ribbon 2½RW (see chart). Follow the directions for the bias Berry. Stitch the center to the middle of the crinoline. Anchor knot and cut the thread.

2. Petals: Fold and gently finger-press the width of the ribbon in half. Pin 5 Boat Gather Petals 1½RW (see chart). Follow Boat Gather Petals through Step 4 to "Match the right sides of the raw edges."

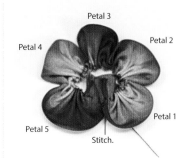

3. Insert the center into the middle of the flower; arrange the petals evenly. Pull the thread tight. Tackstitch the inner gathers of the petals to the crinoline. Anchor knot the thread.

Finished flower

Windflower

Windflower with Deco Leaf-L (page 118). Use ribbon ¼" wider for leaf than for petals.

SKILL LEVEL: **Easy** ◆

Suggested Ribbon

2 different colors of woven or French wire ribbon with a soft or medium hand, double-sided

Amount Needed

- **Center:** 4 × width of Color 1 ribbon
- **Petals:** Approximately 19 × width of Color 2 ribbon plus ½"*

Additional Supplies

- 2RW crinoline circle

Measure and Cut

Ribbon width (RW)	Center: Color 1	Petals: Color 2
	Cut 1 length 4RW.	Measure 3RW per petal.*
1"	4"	3"
⅞"	3½"	2⅝"
¾"	3"	2¼"
⅝"	2½"	1⅞"
½"	2"	1½"
⅜"	1½"	1⅛"

* Do not cut the ribbon until instructed to do so.

DIRECTIONS

See General Directions (page 144), Jelly Roll Center (page 128), and Folded Petals (page 34).

1. Center: Cut 1 length of ribbon 4RW (see chart). Follow the directions for the Jelly Roll Center. Tackstitch the bottom edge of the center into the middle of the crinoline. Anchor knot and cut the thread.

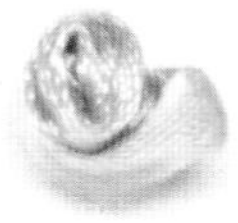

2. Petals: Mark and pin 5 Folded Petals 3RW (see chart). Follow Folded Petals through Step 4 to "Match the right sides of the raw edges."

3. Flower: Insert the center through the middle of the petals. Pull the thread tightly, arranging the petals evenly. Tackstitch the gathered middle of the petals to the crinoline. Anchor knot the thread.

Tackstitch.

Finished flower

Petunia

Petunia with Art Nouveau Leaf-S (page 119). Use same ribbon width for both flower and leaf.

SKILL LEVEL: **Easy** ◆

Suggested Ribbon

Silk bias or woven habotai ribbon

Amount Needed

■ Approximately 15 × width of project ribbon plus ½"*

Additional Supplies

≡ 5 folded stamens

Measure

Ribbon width (RW)	Measure 3RW per petal.*
1"	3"
¾"	2¼"
⅝"	1⅞"
½"	1½"

* Do not cut the ribbon until instructed to do so.

DIRECTIONS

See General Directions (page 144) and Gather and Grab Petals (page 30).

 note

Use the original width of the ribbon to calculate the RW measurements.

1. Mark 5 Gather and Grab Petals 3RW (see chart). Follow Gather and Grab Petals through Step 5 to "Match the right sides of the raw edges."

Stitch.

2. Insert the folded stamens into the center of the flower. Pull the thread tight. Tackstitch. Secure the stamens by wrapping the thread around the raw edges and stamens several times. Anchor the thread.

Tackstitch.

Finished flower

Petunia Brooch

Pansy

Pansy with Oval Leaf-L (with outer edge detail) (page 120). Use ribbon ½" wider for leaf than for flower.

SKILL LEVEL: **Advanced** ◆◆◆

Suggested Ribbon

Silk bias habotai ribbon

Amount Needed

■ Approximately 52 × width of project ribbon plus 1"*

Additional Supplies

■ Silk embroidery ribbon

DIRECTIONS

See General Directions (page 144) and Boat Gather Petals (page 29).

 note

Use the original width of the ribbon to calculate the RW measurements. Where the Boat Gather Petal directions refer to the outer selvage edge, that will be the bias edges in this flower; the inner selvage edge will be the folded edge in this flower.

1. Bottom petals: Fold and gently finger-press the width of the ribbon to ⅝ the original width. Pin 3 Boat Gather Petals in this pattern: 8RW, 12RW, 8RW (see chart). Follow the remaining directions for Boat Gather Petals; do not cut the thread.

2. Beginning at the last petal, stitch through both layers of ribbon. Follow the directions for the outer edge detail stitch (page 143) for each petal. Anchor knot and cut the thread after each petal.

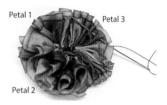

3. Top petals: Follow Step 1 at left. Pin 2 Boat Gather Petals 12RW (see chart); stitch the petals side by side, leaving a large hole in the center to spread the petals out. Follow Step 2 above.

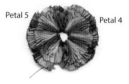

4. Flower: Tackstitch the right side of the top petals to the wrong side of the bottom petals; anchor knot the thread. Stitch a French knot (page 133) in the center of the flower.

Measure

Ribbon width (RW)	Petals	
	Measure 8RW per petal.*	Measure 12RW per petal.*
1"	8"	12"
¾"	6"	9"
⅝"	5"	7½"
½"	4"	6"

* Do not cut the ribbon until instructed to do so.

Bottom petals

Finished flower

Queen's Climber

Queen's Climber with Baroque Leaf (page 122). Use ribbon ¼" wider for leaf than for petals.

SKILL LEVEL: **Intermediate** ◆◆

Suggested Ribbon

2 different colors and widths of woven ribbon with a medium hand, single- or double-sided

Amount Needed

■ **Petals:** 24 × width of Color 1 ribbon

■ **Center:** Approximately 16 × width of Color 2 ribbon plus ½"* (Use ribbon ⅜" narrower than Color 1.)

DIRECTIONS

See General Directions (page 144), Prairie Point Leaf or Petal (page 111), Simple Flower (page 116), and Ruched Petals (page 36).

1. Petals: Cut 8 lengths of ribbon 3RW (see chart). Follow the directions for the Prairie Point Petal for each length; cut the thread. Trim the raw edges down to ¼".

2. Inner layer, 4 petals: Follow Step 2 and Step 5 for the Simple Flower.

3. Outer layer, 4 petals: Follow the directions for the inner layer, pulling the gathers in slightly. Arrange the petals under and in between the inner layer petals.

Tackstitch the outer layer under the inner layer.

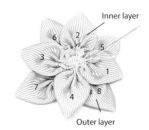

4. Center: Mark 8 Ruched Petals 2RW (see chart). Follow the directions for the Ruched Petal Flower, allowing the petals to lie flat in the middle of the flower.

5. Tackstitch the center to the middle of the flower. Anchor knot the thread.

Finished flower

Measure and Cut

Ribbon width (RW)	Petals: Color 1	Ribbon width (RW)	Center: Color 2
	Cut 8 lengths 3RW.		Measure 2RW per petal.*
1"	3"	⅝"	1¼"
⅞"	2⅝"	½"	1"
¾"	2¼"	⅜"	¾"
⅝"	1⅞"	¼"	½"

* Do not cut the ribbon until instructed to do so.

MINSTREL'S FLOWERS

Kids of all ages stroll down forgotten paths, humming fanciful tunes and looking for nature's delights with open eyes. Here are a few delights that you may have come across in your wanderings, then and now.

The flowers listed in the following chart are accompanied by suggested leaf designs. In some cases, a leaf design is followed by a letter indicating leaf size.

S = Short   **M** = Medium   **L** = Long

For instructions to make the leaves, see Petals, Leaves, and Greenery (page 109).

NEMESIA ... 55
⅝" French wire ribbon and ⅜" grosgrain ribbon with
Baroque Leaf:
⅝" French wire ribbon

YARROW ... 61
2 colors of ⅜" satin ribbon with
Ivy Leaf:
⅝" woven ribbon

HYDRANGEA ... 56
½" and ¼" satin ribbon with
Art Nouveau Leaf-S:
¾" novelty ribbon

FLOWERING QUINCE ... 62
1½" silk bias ribbon with
Bow Tie Leaf:
1½" silk bias ribbon

AMARYLLIS ... 57
⅝" French wire ribbon with
Rooftop Leaf-M:
⅝" French wire ribbon

IRISH ROSE ... 63
¼" satin ribbon with
Sweet Leaf-M:
⅜" taffeta ribbon

COCKLE SHELLS ... 58
1" silk bias ribbon with
Renaissance Leaf-M:
1" silk bias ribbon

WILD ROSE ... 64
1" silk bias ribbon with
Frilly Leaf-M:
1" silk bias ribbon

CUP AND SAUCER VINE ... 59
⅜" and ½" satin ribbon with
Figure 8 Leaf:
⅜" satin ribbon

COLUMBINE ... 65
2 colors of ⅝" satin ribbon with
Notched Leaf-M:
⅝" satin ribbon

DAY LILY ... 60
2 colors of ⅜" satin ribbon with
Baroque Leaf:
⅝" taffeta ribbon

LARKSPUR ... 66
⅜" and ⅝" satin ribbon with
Art Nouveau Leaf-M:
⅝" satin ribbon

Nemesia

Nemesia with Baroque Leaf (page 122). Use same ribbon width for both flower and leaf.

SKILL LEVEL: **Easy** ◆

Suggested Ribbon

2 different colors and widths of woven or French wire ribbon with a soft or medium hand, double-sided

Amount Needed

■ **Center:** 10 × width of Color 1 ribbon

■ **Petals:** Approximately 20 × width of Color 2 ribbon plus ½"* (Use ribbon ¼" wider than Color 1.)

DIRECTIONS

See General Directions (page 144), Single or Double Knot (page 128), and Folded Petals (page 34).

1. Center: Cut 1 length of ribbon 10RW (see chart). Follow the directions for the Double Knot.

2. Petals: Pin 5 Folded Petals in this pattern: 5RW, 2RW, 2RW, 2RW, 5RW (see chart).

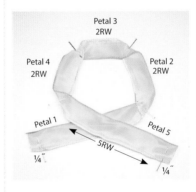

3. Follow Folded Petals through Step 4 to "Match the right sides of the raw edges."

Stitch.

4. Flower: Insert the center into the middle of the petals. Pull the thread tight. Tackstitch and anchor knot into the raw edges.

Tackstitch.

Finished flower

Measure and Cut

Ribbon width (RW)	Center: Color 1	Ribbon width (RW)	Petals: Color 2	
	Cut 1 length 10RW.		Measure 5RW per petal.*	Measure 2RW per petal.*
¾"	7½"	1"	5"	2"
⅝"	6¼"	⅞"	4⅜"	1¾"
½"	5"	¾"	3¾"	1½"
⅜"	3¾"	⅝"	3⅛"	1¼"
¼"	2½"	½"	2½"	1"

* Do not cut the ribbon until instructed to do so.

Hydrangea

Hydrangea with Art Nouveau Leaf-S (page 119). Use ribbon ¼″ wider for leaf than for petals.

SKILL LEVEL: *Intermediate* ◆◆

Suggested Ribbon

2 different colors and widths of woven ribbon with a soft or medium hand, single- or double-sided

Amount Needed

- **Center:** 30 × width of Color 1 ribbon (10RW per flower)
- **Petals:** Approximately 48 × width of Color 2 ribbon plus 1½″* (16RW plus ½″ per flower; use ribbon ¼″ wider than Color 1.)

Additional Supplies

- 4RW square of crinoline

Measure and Cut

Ribbon width (RW)	Center: Color 1	Ribbon width (RW)	Petals: Color 2
	Cut 1 length 10RW.		Measure 4RW per petal.*
¾″	7½″	1″	4″
⅝″	6¼″	⅞″	3½″
½″	5″	¾″	3″
⅜″	3¾″	⅝″	2½″
¼″	2½″	½″	2″

* Do not cut the ribbon until instructed to do so.

DIRECTIONS

See General Directions (page 144), Single or Double Knot (page 128), and Boat Gather Petals (page 29).

1. Center: Cut 1 length of ribbon 10RW (see chart). Follow the directions for the Double Knot.

2. Petals: Mark 4 Boat Gather Petals 4RW (see chart). Follow Boat Gather Petals through Step 4 to "Match the right sides of the raw edges."

3. Flower: Insert the center into the middle of the flower. Pull the thread tight. Tackstitch and anchor knot the thread.

4. Tackstitch the flower to the crinoline. Make 2 more flowers; tackstitch to the crinoline. Trim off the excess crinoline. Make 1 leaf; tackstitch to the wrong side of the crinoline and anchor knot the thread.

Finished group

Amaryllis

Amaryllis with Rooftop Leaf-M (page 114). Use same ribbon width for both flower and leaf.

SKILL LEVEL: *Intermediate* ◊ ◊

Suggested Ribbon

Woven or French wire ribbon with a medium to stiff hand, single- or double-sided

Amount Needed

- 24 × width of project ribbon

Additional Supplies

- 5 folded stamens

Measure and Cut

Ribbon width (RW)	Cut 6 lengths 4RW.
1"	4"
⅞"	3½"
¾"	3"
⅝"	2½"
½"	2"
⅜"	1½"

DIRECTIONS

See General Directions (page 144), Miter Fold Leaf or Petal (page 115), and Simple Flower (page 116).

1. Petals: Cut 6 lengths of ribbon 4RW (see chart). Follow the directions for the Miter Fold Petal for each length. Anchor knot and cut the thread.

2. Flower: Follow Steps 2–4 for the Simple Flower, inserting the stamens into the middle of the flower in Step 3. Secure the stamens by wrapping the thread around the raw edges and stamens several times. Anchor the thread.

Finished flower

Cockle Shells

Cockle Shells with Renaissance Leaf-M (page 117). Use same ribbon width for both flower and leaf.

SKILL LEVEL: *Intermediate* ◆◆

Suggested Ribbon

Silk bias or woven habotai ribbon

Amount Needed

■ 12 × original width of project ribbon

Additional Supplies

■ 3 folded stamens

Measure and Cut

Ribbon width (RW)	Cut 1 length 12RW.
1″	12″
¾″	9″
⅝″	7½″
½″	6″
7/16″	5¼″

DIRECTIONS

See General Directions (page 144) and Posy (page 26).

 note

Use the original width of the ribbon to calculate the RW measurements. Where the Posy directions refer to the outer selvage edge, that will be the bias edges in this flower; the inner selvage edge will be the folded edge in this flower.

1. Cut 1 length of ribbon 12RW (see chart). Fold and gently finger-press the right end of the ribbon to almost half the original width; taper the fold down to ⅛″ at the left end. Place pins ½RW from each end and throughout the length to hold the fold in place.

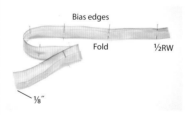

Bias edges

Fold   ½RW

⅛″

2. Follow the stitch directions in Steps 1–3 for the Posy.

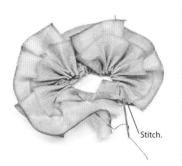

Stitch.

3. Insert the stamens into the middle of the flower. Follow Step 4. Tackstitch and anchor knot but do not cut the thread.

4. Beginning at the shorter end, stitch through both layers of ribbon. Follow the directions for the outer edge detail stitch (page 143). Anchor knot the thread.

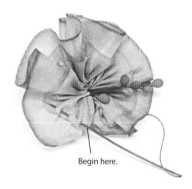

Begin here.

Finished flower

Cup and Saucer Vine

Cup and Saucer Vine with Figure 8 Leaf (page 124). Use same ribbon width for both center and leaf.

SKILL LEVEL: *Intermediate* ◆◆

Suggested Ribbon

2 different colors and widths of woven ribbon with a soft or medium hand, single- or double-sided

Amount Needed

▪ **Bulb:** 8 × width of Color 1 ribbon

▪ **Center:** Color 2 ribbon (Use ribbon ⅛" narrower than Color 1 in same length.)

Additional Supplies

▪ 3 folded stamens
▪ Small amount of stuffing

Measure and Cut

Ribbon width (RW)	Cut 1 length 8RW from Color 1.
1"	8"
⅞"	7"
¾"	6"
⅝"	5"
½"	4"
⅜"	3"

DIRECTIONS

See General Directions (page 144), Inner Edge Layering (page 16), Rosette (page 25), and Berry and Stuffed Berry (page 131).

1. Cut 1 length of ribbon 8RW (see chart) from Color 1. Follow the directions for inner edge layering, with the narrower ribbon on top of the wider ribbon. Follow Steps 1 and 2 for the Rosette, stitching through both layers of ribbon.

2. Follow Step 3, inserting the stamens into the middle of the flower. Wrap the thread around the stamens several times. Anchor knot the thread.

3. Working on the selvage edge of the wider ribbon, follow the gather stitch directions in Step 2 for the Stuffed Berry.

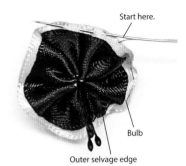

4. Gently pull the 2 ribbons apart. Follow the stuffing directions. Pull the thread firmly to close the center opening. Tackstitch and anchor knot the thread.

Stuff bulb.

Finished flower

Day Lily

Day Lily with Baroque Leaf (page 122). Use ribbon ¼" wider for leaf than for petals.

SKILL LEVEL: **Intermediate** ◆◆

Suggested Ribbon

2 different colors of woven ribbon with a soft or medium hand, double-sided

Amount Needed

▪ **Inner petals:** Approximately 24 × width of Color 1 ribbon

▪ **Outer petals:** 30 × width of Color 2 ribbon

▪ **Center:** Approximately 16 × width of Color 2 ribbon plus ½"*

Additional Supplies

▪ 2RW crinoline circle

Measure and Cut

Ribbon width (RW)	Inner petals: Color 1	Outer petals: Color 2	Center: Color 2
	Cut 6 lengths 4RW.	Cut 6 lengths 5RW.	Measure 8 petals 2RW each.*
1"	4"	5"	2"
⅞"	3½"	4⅜"	1¾"
¾"	3"	3¾"	1½"
⅝"	2½"	3⅛"	1¼"
½"	2"	2½"	1"
⅜"	1½"	1⅞"	¾"

Do not cut the ribbon until instructed to do so.

DIRECTIONS

See General Directions (page 144), Soft Curve Leaf or Petal (page 111), Simple Flower (page 116), and Ruched Petals (page 36).

1. Petals: Cut 6 lengths of ribbon 4RW from Color 1 (see chart); cut 6 lengths of ribbon 5RW from Color 2 (see chart). Group these into pairs. Follow the directions for a Soft Curve Petal, reversing the direction of the fold, for a pair with Color 1 on top. Repeat for each pair.

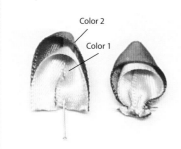

2. Flower: Follow Steps 2 and 5 of the Simple Flower. Tackstitch the raw edges to the crinoline. Anchor knot and cut the thread.

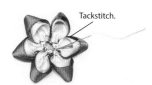
Tackstitch.

3. Center: Mark 8 Ruched Petals 2RW (see chart). Follow the directions for Ruched Petals, allowing the petals to lie flat in the middle of the flower. Tackstitch the center to the crinoline, covering the raw edges of the flower. Anchor knot the thread.

Tackstitch.

Finished flower

Yarrow

Yarrow with Ivy Leaf (page 121). Use ribbon ¼″ wider for leaf than for flower.

SKILL LEVEL: *Intermediate* ◆◆

Suggested Ribbon

2 different colors of woven ribbon with a soft or medium hand, single- or double-sided

Amount Needed

▪ **Outer petals:** Approximately 24 × width of Color 1 ribbon plus ½″*

▪ **Center petals:** Approximately 24 × width of Color 2 ribbon plus ½″*

Additional Supplies

▪ 3RW crinoline circle

DIRECTIONS

See General Directions (page 144) and Ruched Petals (page 36).

1. Outer petals: Mark 8 Ruched Petals 3RW (see chart). Follow Ruched Petals through Step 4.

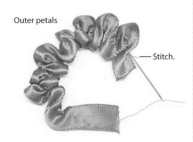

Outer petals

Stitch.

2. Match the right sides of the raw edges together. Pull the thread gently, leaving a small opening in the middle of the flower. Arrange the petals flat with the raw edges facing in. Tackstitch the inner lobes to the crinoline. Anchor knot and cut the thread.

3. Center petals: Mark 16 Ruched Petals, alternating between 1RW and 2RW lengths (see chart). Follow the remaining directions for Ruched Petals, allowing the petals to lie flat in the center.

4. Flower: Tackstitch the inner petals of the center to the crinoline. Anchor knot the thread.

Tackstitch.

Finished flower

Measure

Ribbon width (RW)	Outer petals: Color 1	Center petals: Color 2	
	Measure 3RW per petal.*	Measure 1RW per petal.*	Measure 2RW per petal.*
1″	3″	1″	2″
⅞″	2⅝″	⅞″	1¾″
¾″	2¼″	¾″	1½″
⅝″	1⅞″	⅝″	1¼″
½″	1½″	½″	1″
⅜″	1⅛″	⅜″	¾″

* Do not cut the ribbon until instructed to do so.

Flowering Quince

Flowering Quince with Bow Tie Leaf (page 124). Use same ribbon width for both flower and leaf.

SKILL LEVEL: **Intermediate** ◆◆

Suggested Ribbon

Silk bias ribbon: habotai, satin, or velvet

Amount Needed

■ 5 × width of project ribbon

Additional Supplies

■ 5 folded stamens

DIRECTIONS

See General Directions (page 144).

1. Cut 5 lengths of ribbon 1RW for the petals. Fold each petal in half diagonally; pin each folded corner. The 3 points of the petal will be labeled A, B, and C. Place the first petal with the fold as shown.

 note

The fold of the petal will always be placed in the center; stitching will be along the bias edges.

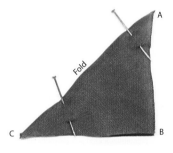

2. Place the next petal on top of the first, matching points A to B and B to C of the previous petal; pin through all the layers.

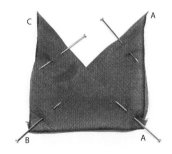

3. Repeat for each remaining petal, attaching petal 1 under petal 5. Each corner will have 3 layers of petals. Anchor knot the thread into a corner as shown.

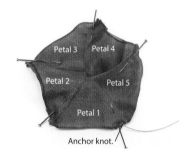

Anchor knot.

4. Gather stitch through all the layers of ribbon, ⅛" above the cut and bias edges, beginning at the anchor knot and ending just before the beginning anchor knot.

Begin.

End stitching before beginning anchor knot.

5. Pull the gathers in slightly to form the center of the flower; insert the stamens into the middle of the flower. Pull the thread tight. Tackstitch and anchor knot the thread.

Tackstitch.

Finished flower

Irish Rose

Irish Rose with Sweet Leaf-M (page 117). Use ribbon ⅛" wider for leaf than for flower.

SKILL LEVEL: **Advanced** ◆◆◆

Suggested Ribbon

Woven ribbon with a soft, medium, or stiff hand, double-sided

Amount Needed

▪ Approximately 168 × width of project ribbon plus 1½"*

Additional Supplies

▪ 4RW crinoline circle

Measure

Ribbon width (RW)	Measure 4RW per petal.*
1"	4"
⅞"	3½"
¾"	3"
⅝"	2½"
½"	2"
⅜"	1½"
¼"	1"

* Do not cut the ribbon until instructed to do so.

DIRECTIONS

See General Directions (page 144) and Hop 'n Stitch Petals (page 32).

1. Center petals: Mark 8 Hop 'n Stitch Petals 4RW (see chart). Follow the remaining directions for Hop 'n Stitch Petals, allowing the petals to face upward. Tackstitch the center to the crinoline. Anchor knot and cut the thread.

2. Middle petals: Mark 14 Hop 'n Stitch Petals 4RW (see chart). Follow the directions for Hop 'n Stitch Petals through Step 3.

3. Insert the center petals into the opening of the middle petals. Pull the thread tightly, arranging the petals evenly and facing up. Tuck the raw edges under the middle petals.

Tackstitch the gathered edge of the inner layer to the crinoline. Anchor knot and cut the thread. Arrange the petals facing up.

Tackstitch.

4. Outer petals: Mark 20 Hop 'n Stitch Petals 4RW (see chart). Repeat Steps 2 and 3 at left and above. Anchor knot the thread.

Tackstitch.

Finished flower

Wild Rose

Wild Rose with Frilly Leaf-M (page 121). Use same ribbon width for both petals and leaf.

SKILL LEVEL: *Intermediate* ◆◆

Suggested Ribbon

2 different colors and widths of silk bias habotai ribbon

Amount Needed

- **Petals:** Approximately 25 × width of Color 1 ribbon plus ½"*
- **Center:** 3 × width of Color 2 ribbon (Use ribbon approximately ⅜" narrower than Color 1.)

Measure and Cut

Ribbon width (RW)	Petals: Color 1	Ribbon width (RW)	Center: Color 2
	Measure 5RW per petal.*		Cut 1 length 3RW.
1"	5"	⅝"	1⅞"
¾"	3¾"	⁷⁄₁₆"	1⁵⁄₁₆"

* Do not cut the ribbon until instructed to do so.

DIRECTIONS

See General Directions (page 144), Gather and Grab Petals (page 30), and Berry and Stuffed Berry (page 131).

 note

> Use the original width of the ribbon to calculate the RW measurements.

1. Petals: Fold and gently finger-press the width of the ribbon to ⅝ the original width. Pin 5 Gather and Grab Petals 5RW (see chart). Follow the remaining directions for Gather and Grab Petals. Anchor knot the thread.

2. Beginning at the first petal, follow the directions for the outer edge detail stitch (page 143), stitching through both layers of ribbon. Anchor knot the thread. Repeat for each remaining petal. Anchor knot and cut the thread.

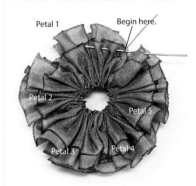

3. Center: Cut 1 length of ribbon 3RW (see chart). Follow the directions for the bias Berry; do not cut the thread.

4. Flower: Tackstitch the center to the middle of the petals.

Finished flower

Columbine

Columbine with Notched Leaf-M (page 120). Use same ribbon width for both flower and leaf.

SKILL LEVEL: *Advanced* ◆◆◆

Suggested Ribbon

2 different colors of woven or French wire ribbon with a soft or medium hand, single- or double-sided

Amount Needed

▪ **Inner petals:** Approximately 10 × width of Color 1 ribbon plus ½"*

▪ **Outer petals:** 20 × width of Color 2 ribbon

Additional Supplies

▪ 3 folded stamens

Measure and Cut

Ribbon width (RW)	Inner petals: Color 1	Outer petals: Color 2
	Measure 2RW per petal.*	Cut 5 lengths 4RW.
1"	2"	4"
⅞"	1¾"	3½"
¾"	1½"	3"
⅝"	1¼"	2½"
½"	1"	2"
⅜"	¾"	1½"

* Do not cut the ribbon until instructed to do so.

DIRECTIONS

See General Directions (page 144), Boat Gather Petals (page 29), Calla Lily (page 45), General Assembly Directions (page 110), and Simple Flower (page 116).

1. Inner petals: Mark 5 Boat Gather Petals 2RW (see chart). Follow Boat Gather Petals through Step 4 to "Match the right sides of the raw edges." Insert the stamens into the middle of the inner petals. Pull the thread tight. Tackstitch. Anchor knot and cut the thread.

2. Outer petals: Cut 5 lengths of ribbon 4RW (see chart). Working with 1 length, follow Steps 1 and 2 for the Calla Lily (omitting the stamen in Step 2). Follow Step 3, but tackstitch at the raw edges; then repeat for the right side.

Follow Steps 2–4 of General Assembly Directions; cut the thread. Repeat for each length.

Left side — Right side

Tackstitch here.

3. Flower: Follow Step 2 for the Simple Flower.

4. Follow Steps 3 and 4 for the Simple Flower, inserting the inner petals into the middle of the flower in Step 3.

Finished flower

Larkspur

Larkspur with Art Nouveau Leaf-M (page 119). Use same ribbon width for both leaf and outer petals.

SKILL LEVEL: *Intermediate* ◆◆

Suggested Ribbon

2 different colors and sizes of woven ribbon with a soft or medium hand, double-sided

Amount Needed

- **Outer petals:** Approximately 23 × width of Color 1 ribbon plus ½"*
- **Inner petals:** Approximately 22 × width of Color 2 ribbon plus ½"* (Use ribbon ¼" narrower than Color 1.)

Additional Supplies

- 5 folded stamens
- 2RW crinoline circle

Measure

Ribbon width (RW)	Outer petals: Color 1	Ribbon width (RW)	Inner petals: Color 2
	Measure 2RW per petal.*		Measure 2RW per petal.*
1"	2"	¾"	1½"
⅞"	1¾"	⅝"	1¼"
¾"	1½"	½"	1"
⅝"	1¼"	⅜"	¾"
½"	1"	¼"	½"

* Do not cut the ribbon until instructed to do so.

DIRECTIONS

See General Directions (page 144), Folded Petals (page 34), and Gala Gather Petals (page 31).

1. Outer petals: Pin 8 Folded Petals 2RW (see chart). Follow Folded Petals through Step 4, leaving an opening in the middle of the flower approximately 1RW. Tackstitch the center gathers to the crinoline. Anchor knot and cut the thread.

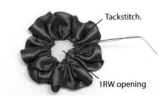

Tackstitch.

1RW opening

2. Inner petals: Mark 11 Gala Gather Petals 2RW (see chart). Follow Gala Gather Petals through Step 4 to "Match the right sides of the raw edges."

3. Insert the stamens into the middle of the flower. Follow the remaining directions for Gala Gather Petals. Anchor knot but do not cut the thread. Tuck the folded ends of the stamens under the center. Tackstitch in place.

4. Tackstitch the inner petals of the center to the crinoline, in the middle of the outer petals. Anchor knot the thread.

Finished flower

SUMMER FLOWERS

A robin's song fills the soft summer morning air, as last night's dew still kisses delicately scented petals. The long days of summer are cherished because of the variety and color that nature offers us. Here are a few blooms for you to enjoy.

The flowers listed in the following chart are accompanied by suggested leaf designs. In some cases, a leaf design is followed by a letter indicating leaf size.

S = Short   **M** = Medium   **L** = Long

For instructions to make the leaves, see Petals, Leaves, and Greenery (page 109).

DOUBLE DAISY ... 69
1" and ⅝" silk bias ribbon with
Renaissance Leaf-M:
1" silk bias ribbon

GRAND DUCHESS ... 75
½" and ⅜" satin ribbons with
Baroque Leaf:
⅝" satin ribbon

ANGEL WING BEGONIA ... 70
⅜" satin ribbon with
Winged Leaf:
⅝" satin ribbon

CAMPION ... 76
⅜" satin ribbon and ¼" taffeta
ribbon with *Neapolitan Leaf-L:*
⅜" woven ribbon

SWEET ALYSSUM ... 71
2 colors of ⅜" satin ribbon with
Notched Leaf-M:
⅜" satin ribbon

IMPATIENS ... 77
1" silk bias ribbon with
Oval Leaf-M:
1" silk bias ribbon

**ESTRELLA WITH SILK
CENTER ... 72**
1½" silk bias ribbon with
Frilly Leaf-M:
1½" silk bias ribbon

ROSIE RAMBLER ... 78
¾" silk satin ribbon and ⅝" satin
ribbon *with Ivy Leaf:*
⅝" satin ribbon

PENNINE MUM ... 73
⅜" and ½" satin ribbon with
Sweet Leaf-M:
⅜" taffeta ribbon

EMPRESS LILY ... 79
1" silk satin ribbon with
Neapolitan Leaf-L:
1" French wire ribbon

CHRYSANTHEMUM ... 74
⅝" satin ribbon with
Neapolitan Leaf-M:
⅝" satin ribbon

PINCUSHION FLOWER ... 80
⅜" and ½" satin ribbon with
Pinch Tip Leaf-M:
⅜" satin ribbon

Double Daisy

Double Daisy with Renaissance Leaf-M (page 117). Use same ribbon width for both outer petals and leaf.

SKILL LEVEL: *Intermediate* ◆◆

Suggested Ribbon

2 different colors and widths of silk bias habotai ribbon

Amount Needed

■ **Outer layer:** 12 × width of Color 1 ribbon

■ **Inner layer:** 12 × width of Color 2 ribbon (Use ribbon approximately ½" narrower than Color 1.)

Additional Supplies

■ Silk embroidery ribbon

DIRECTIONS

See General Directions (page 144) and Rosette (page 25).

 note

Use the original width of the ribbon to calculate the RW measurements. Where the directions for the Rosette refer to the outer selvage edge, that will be the bias edges in this flower; the inner selvage edge will be the folded edge in this flower.

1. Outer layer: Cut 1 length of ribbon 12RW (see chart). Fold and gently finger-press the width of the ribbon to ⅝ the original width. Fold the length of ribbon in half, matching the raw edges, folded edges, and bias edges. Follow the seam directions in Step 1 for the Rosette.

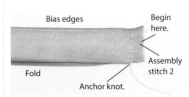

2. Open the ribbon to the right side; follow the remaining directions for Rosette, stitching through both layers along the fold. Anchor knot and cut the thread.

3. Inner layer: Cut 1 length of ribbon 12RW (see chart). Repeat Steps 1 and 2 at left and above.

4. Tackstitch the inner layer on top of the outer layer. Stitch a French knot (page 133) in the center of the inner layer.

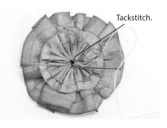

Finished flower

Measure and Cut

Ribbon width (RW)	Outer layer: Color 1	Ribbon width (RW)	Inner layer: Color 2
	Cut 1 length 12RW.		Cut 1 length 12RW.
1"	12"	⅝"	7½"
¾"	9"	⁷⁄₁₆"	5¼"

Angel Wing Begonia

Angel Wing Begonia with Winged Leaf (page 123). Use ribbon ¼" wider for leaf than for flower.

SKILL LEVEL: **Easy** ◈

Suggested Ribbon

Woven or French wire ribbon with a soft, medium, or stiff hand, double-sided

Amount Needed

- Approximately 36 × width of project ribbon plus 1½"* (12RW plus ½" per flower)

Additional Supplies

- 15 folded stamens (5 per flower)
- 4RW square of crinoline

Measure

Ribbon width (RW)	Measure 4RW per petal.*	Measure 2RW per petal.*
1"	4"	2"
⅞"	3½"	1¾"
¾"	3"	1½"
⅝"	2½"	1¼"
½"	2"	1"
⅜"	1½"	¾"

* Do not cut the ribbon until instructed to do so.

DIRECTIONS

See General Directions (page 144) and Gala Gather Petals (page 31).

1. Mark 4 Gala Gather Petals in this pattern: 4RW, 2RW, 4RW, 2RW (see chart). Follow the gather stitch directions for Gala Gather Petals through Step 3.

Gently pull in the gathers, arranging the petals flat, with petals 2 and 4 under petals 1 and 3. From behind, stitch through the selvage edge next to the starting anchor knot.

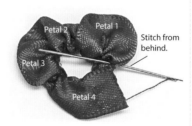

2. Thread the needle back through the middle to the wrong side of the flower. Insert the stamens into the middle of the flower. Pull the thread tight.

Tackstitch and anchor knot the thread.

Tackstitch.

Finished flower

3. Tackstitch the flower to the crinoline.

4. Make 2 more flowers. Tackstitch to the crinoline in a cluster. Make 1 leaf. Tackstitch on top of the crinoline, covering any exposed stamen ends. Anchor knot the thread. Trim off the excess crinoline.

Finished group

Sweet Alyssum

Sweet Alyssum with Notched Leaf-M (page 120). Use same ribbon width for both flower and leaf.

SKILL LEVEL: *Intermediate* ◆◆

Suggested Ribbon

2 different colors of woven ribbon with a soft or medium hand, double-sided

Amount Needed

■ **Center:** 30 × width of Color 1 ribbon (10RW per flower)

■ **Petals:** Approximately 27 × width of Color 2 ribbon plus 1½"* (9RW plus ½" per flower.)

Additional Supplies

■ 4RW square of crinoline

Measure and Cut

Ribbon width (RW)	Center: Color 1	Petals: Color 2
	Cut 1 length 10RW.	Measure 1RW per petal.*
1"	10"	1"
⅞"	8¾"	⅞"
¾"	7½"	¾"
⅝"	6¼"	⅝"
½"	5"	½"
⅜"	3¾"	⅜"

Do not cut the ribbon until instructed to do so.

DIRECTIONS

See General Directions (page 144), Single or Double Knot (page 128), and Flip 'n Fold Petals (page 38).

1. Center: Cut 1 length of ribbon 10RW. Follow the directions for the Double Knot.

2. Petals: Follow Steps 1–4 for the Flip 'n Fold petals, stitching a total of 8 petals.

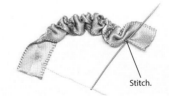

Stitch.

3. Follow Step 5, inserting the center into the middle of the flower. Follow the remaining directions. Tackstitch the raw edges of the flower to the center.

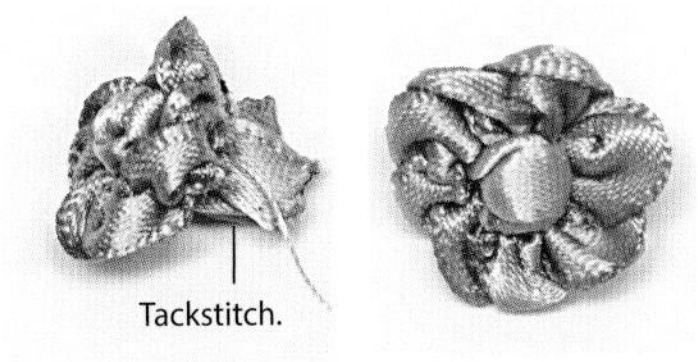

Tackstitch.

Finished flower

4. Tackstitch the flower to the crinoline. Make 2 more flowers; tackstitch to the crinoline. Trim off the excess crinoline. Make 1 leaf; tackstitch to the wrong side of the crinoline and anchor knot the thread.

Finished group

Estrella with Silk Center

Estrella with Silk Center and Frilly Leaf-M (page 121). Use same ribbon width for both flower and leaf.

Suggested Ribbon

Silk bias ribbon: habotai or satin

Amount Needed

- 7 × width of project ribbon

DIRECTIONS

See General Directions (page 144), Bandana Fold Leaf or Petal (page 114), and Simple Flower (page 116).

Silk Center

1. Cut 1 piece of ribbon 1RW. Anchor knot the thread into a corner, ⅛" from the bias edge. Gather stitch around the entire outer edge, coming back to the beginning stitch (but not overlapping it). Pull in the gathers to form the center. Tackstitch and anchor knot the thread.

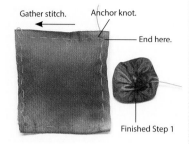

Gather stitch. Anchor knot.

End here.

Finished Step 1

2. Gather stitch around the new folded outer edge, stitching through both layers. Pull in the gathers. Anchor knot but do not cut the thread.

Start here.

Finished Step 2

Flower

1. Follow Step 1 for Bandana Fold Petals; cut 6 petals. Anchor knot the thread into the folded edge of the first petal, ⅛" from the raw edge. Gather stitch across the width of the ribbon, beginning with the needle on the top side of the ribbon and ending with the needle on the underside of the ribbon.

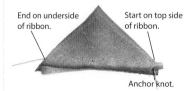

End on underside of ribbon. Start on top side of ribbon.

Anchor knot.

2. Repeat for each petal, causing the petals to overlap slightly as you stitch. Stitch through the top side of the folded edge of the first petal, next to the beginning anchor knot.

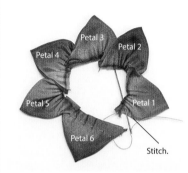

Petal 3 Petal 2 Petal 4 Petal 1 Petal 5 Petal 6 Stitch.

3. Follow Step 5 for the Simple Flower. Stitch the silk center into the middle of the petals. Tackstitch and anchor knot the thread.

Silk center

Finished flower

Pennine Mum

Pennine Mum with Sweet Leaf-M (page 117). Use same ribbon width for both outer petals and leaf.

SKILL LEVEL: *Intermediate* ◆◆

Suggested Ribbon

2 different colors and widths of woven ribbon with a soft or medium hand, single- or double-sided

Amount Needed

▪ **Outer petals:** Approximately 42 × width of Color 1 ribbon plus ½"*

▪ **Center:** Approximately 26 × width of Color 2 ribbon plus ½"* (Use ribbon ⅛" wider than Color 1.)

Additional Supplies

▪ 2RW crinoline circle

Measure

Ribbon width (RW)	Outer petals: Color 1	Ribbon width (RW)	Center: Color 2
	Measure 3RW per petal.*		Measure 1RW per petal.*
⅞"	2⅝"	1"	1"
¾"	2¼"	⅞"	⅞"
⅝"	1⅞"	¾"	¾"
½"	1½"	⅝"	⅝"
⅜"	1⅛"	½"	½"

* Do not cut the ribbon until instructed to do so.

DIRECTIONS

See General Directions (page 144), Ruched Petals (page 36), and Pouf Gather Center (page 132).

1. Outer petals: Mark 14 Ruched Petals 3RW (see chart). Follow Ruched Petals through Step 5 to "Match the right sides of the raw edges."

Stitch.

2. Pull in the gathers, leaving the lobes flat with a 1RW opening in the middle of the petals. Tackstitch the inner lobes to the crinoline. Anchor knot and cut the thread.

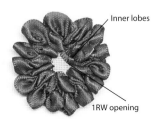
Inner lobes
1RW opening

3. Center: Mark 13 Pouf Gather Petals 1RW (see chart). Follow the remaining directions. Anchor knot the thread.

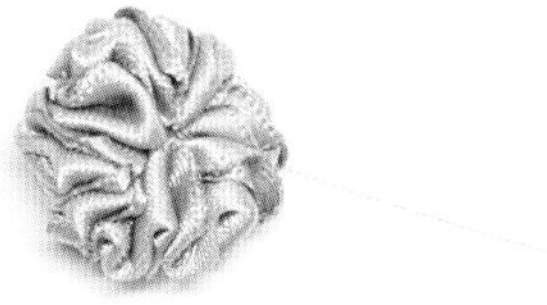

4. Flower: Tackstitch the center to the middle of the flower. Anchor knot the thread into the crinoline.

Tackstitch.

Finished flower

Chrysanthemum

Chrysanthemum with Neapolitan Leaf-M (page 118). Use the same ribbon width for both flower and leaf.

SKILL LEVEL: *Intermediate* ◆◆

Suggested Ribbon

Woven ribbon with a soft or medium hand, single- or double-sided

Amount Needed

- 35 × width of project ribbon

Additional Supplies

- 2RW crinoline circle

Measure and Cut

Ribbon width (RW)	Center	Inner layer	Outer layer
	Cut 1 length 10RW.	Cut 1 length 9RW.	Cut 1 length 16RW.
1″	10″	9″	16″
⅞″	8¾″	7⅞″	14″
¾″	7½″	6¾″	12″
⅝″	6¼″	5⅝″	10″
½″	5″	4½″	8″
⅜″	3¾″	3⅜″	6″

DIRECTIONS

See General Directions (page 144), Single or Double Knot (page 128), and Ruffled Rosette (page 129).

1. Center: Cut 1 length of ribbon 10RW (see chart). Follow the directions for the Double Knot (not shown).

2. Inner layer: Cut 1 length of ribbon 9RW (see chart). Follow the directions for the Ruffled Rosette through Step 2, stitching through both layers of ribbon.

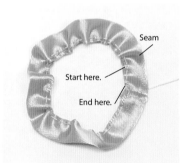

3. Gently pull the thread to form the middle of the inner layer. Insert the center into the middle of the inner layer. Tackstitch and anchor knot the thread. Cut the raw edges of the center down to ¼″.

4. Tackstitch the inner layer to the crinoline, stitching around the inner gathers. Anchor knot and cut the thread.

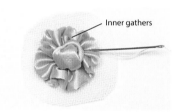

5. Outer layer: Cut 1 length of ribbon 16RW (see chart). Repeat Steps 2 and 3 at left and above, inserting the inner layer into the middle of the outer layer in Step 3. Repeat Step 4 above, stitching around the inner gathers of the outer layer.

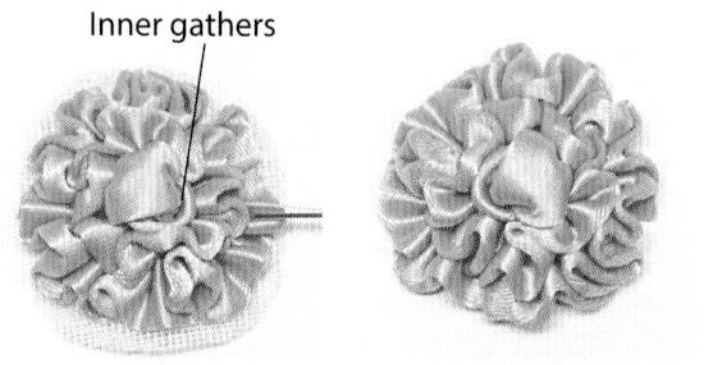

Finished flower

Grand Duchess

Grand Duchess with Baroque Leaf (page 122). Use ribbon ⅛" wider for leaf than for outer petals.

SKILL LEVEL: **Intermediate** ◆◆

Suggested Ribbon

2 different colors and widths of woven ribbon with a soft or medium hand, single- or double-sided

Amount Needed

- **Outer petals and center:** 41 × width of Color 1 ribbon plus ½"

- **Inner petals:** 32 × width of Color 2 ribbon (Use ribbon ⅛" narrower than Color 1.)

Measure and Cut

Ribbon width (RW)	Outer petals and center: Color 1		Ribbon width (RW)	Inner petals: Color 2
	Cut 8 lengths 4RW.	Cut 1 length 9RW plus ½".		Cut 8 lengths 4RW.
1"	4"	9½"	⅞"	3½"
⅞"	3½"	8⅜"	¾"	3"
¾"	3"	7¼"	⅝"	2½"
⅝"	2½"	6⅛"	½"	2"
½"	2"	5"	⅜"	1½"
⅜"	1½"	3⅞"	¼"	1"

DIRECTIONS

See General Directions (page 144), Rooftop Leaf or Petal (page 114), Simple Flower (page 116), and Knotted Posy and Knotted Ruffled Posy (page 27).

1. Petals: Cut 8 lengths 4RW from each ribbon color (see chart); group these into pairs. Follow the fold and pin directions for Rooftop Petals for each length. Working with 1 pair, place the narrower width on top of the wider width; follow the remaining directions. Repeat for each pair.

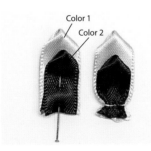

Color 1
Color 2

2. Follow Steps 2 and 5 for the Simple Flower.

3. Center: Cut 1 length of ribbon 9RW plus ½" (see chart). Follow the directions for the Knotted Ruffled Posy.

4. Flower: Tackstitch the center into the middle of the petals. Anchor knot the thread.

Tackstitch.

Finished flower

Campion

Campion with Neapolitan Leaf-L (page 118). Use same ribbon width for both petals and leaf.

SKILL LEVEL: *Easy* ◆

Suggested Ribbon

2 different colors and widths of woven ribbon with a soft or medium hand, single- or double-sided

Amount Needed

▪ **Petals:** Approximately 36 × width of Color 1 ribbon plus 1"*

▪ **Center:** 8 × width of Color 2 ribbon (Use ribbon ⅛" narrower than Color 1.)

Measure and Cut

Ribbon width (RW)	Outer petals: Color 1	Inner petals: Color 1	Ribbon width (RW)	Center: Color 2
	Measure 5RW per petal.*	Measure 4RW per petal.*		Cut 1 length 8RW.
1"	5"	4"	⅞"	7"
⅞"	4⅜"	3½"	¾"	6"
¾"	3¾"	3"	⅝"	5"
⅝"	3⅛"	2½"	½"	4"
½"	2½"	2"	⅜"	3"
⅜"	1⅞"	1½"	¼"	2"

* Do not cut the ribbon until instructed to do so.

DIRECTIONS

See General Directions (page 144), Star Point Petals (page 33), and Rosette (page 25).

1. Outer petals: Mark 4 Star Point Petals 5RW (see chart). Follow the directions to make a Star Point Petal Flower. Anchor knot and cut the thread.

2. Inner petals: Mark 4 Star Point Petals 4RW (see chart). Follow Step 1 above. Anchor knot but do not cut the thread.

3. Arrange the outer petals under and in between the inner petals. Tackstitch through the center gathers. Anchor knot and cut the thread.

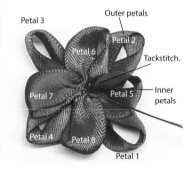

4. Center: Cut 1 length of ribbon 8RW (see chart). Follow the directions for the Rosette. Tackstitch the center to the middle of the inner petals. Anchor knot the thread.

Finished flower

Impatiens

Impatiens with Oval Leaf-M (page 120). Use same ribbon width for both flower and leaf.

SKILL LEVEL: *Intermediate* ◆◆

Suggested Ribbon

Silk bias ribbon: habotai, satin, or velvet

Amount Needed

▪ 6 × width of project ribbon

Additional Supplies

▪ Silk embroidery ribbon (optional)

DIRECTIONS

See General Directions (page 144) and Estrella with Silk Center (page 72).

1. Petals: Cut 5 lengths of ribbon 1RW. Fold each petal in half diagonally; pin each folded corner. The 3 points of the petal will be labeled A, B, and C. Place the first petal with the fold away from you.

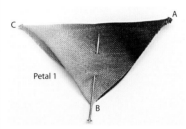

2. Place the next petal on top of the previous petal, matching points C to A, and B to B; pin through all the layers. Anchor knot the thread close to point B through all the layers of ribbon. Gather stitch through all the layers of ribbon to the folds.

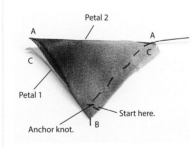

3. Slightly pull the gathers to form a curved spine. Anchor knot the thread into the raw edges.

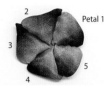

4. Repeat for each remaining petal, connecting the last petal with the first. Anchor knot and cut the thread.

5. Center: Cut 1 length of ribbon 1RW. Follow the directions for the Silk Center. Stitch this into the center of the flower. *Optional:* You can make the center using a French knot (page 133) instead.

Finished flowers with silk center (1) and French knot (2)

Rosie Rambler

Rosie Rambler with Ivy Leaf (page 121). Use same ribbon width for both petals and leaf.

SKILL LEVEL: *Intermediate* ◆◆

Suggested Ribbon

2 different colors and widths of woven ribbon with a soft or medium hand, double-sided

Amount Needed

▪ **Petals:** Approximately 13 × width of Color 1 ribbon plus ½"*

▪ **Center:** Approximately 5 × width of Color 2 ribbon* (Use ribbon ⅛" wider than Color 1.)

Additional Supplies

▪ 2RW crinoline circle

* Do not cut the ribbon until instructed to do so.

DIRECTIONS

See General Directions (page 144), Flip 'n Fold Petals (page 38), and Rose Bud Center (page 130).

1. Petals: Follow the directions for the Flip 'n Fold Petals through Step 4, stitching 12 petals.

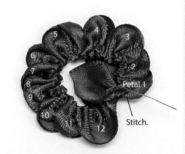

2. Follow Step 5, leaving a 1RW opening in the center of the flower. Place the raw edges into the middle of the petals. Tackstitch the inner gathers to the crinoline. Anchor knot and cut the thread.

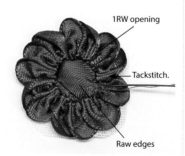

3. Center: Follow the directions for the Rose Bud Center.

4. Flower: Tackstitch the center into the middle of the flower. Tackstitch each lobe of the center to the crinoline. Anchor knot the thread.

Finished flower

Empress Lily

Empress Lily with Neapolitan Leaf-L (page 118). Use same ribbon width for both flower and leaf.

SKILL LEVEL: *Intermediate* ◆◆

Suggested Ribbon

2 different colors of woven or French wire ribbon with a soft or medium hand, double-sided

Amount Needed

▪ **Petals:** 18 × width of Color 1 ribbon

▪ **Calyx:** 6 × width of Color 2 ribbon

Additional Supplies

▪ 5 folded stamens

Measure and Cut

Ribbon width (RW)	Petals: Color 1	Calyx: Color 2
	Cut 6 lengths 3RW.	Cut 1 length 6RW.
1″	3″	6″
⅞″	2⅝″	5¼″
¾″	2¼″	4½″
⅝″	1⅞″	3¾″
½″	1½″	3″

DIRECTIONS

See General Directions (page 144), Prairie Point Leaf or Petal (page 111), Simple Flower (page 116), and Berry and Stuffed Berry (page 131).

1. Petals: Cut 6 lengths of ribbon 3RW (see chart). Follow the directions for the Prairie Point Petal for each length. Anchor knot and cut the thread.

2. Flower: Follow Steps 2–4 for the Simple Flower, inserting the stamens into the middle of the flower in Step 3. Anchor knot and cut the thread.

3. Calyx: Cut 1 length of ribbon 6RW (see chart). Follow Steps 1 and 2 for the Berry.

4. Insert the raw edges of the flower into the opening of the calyx. Gently pull the thread to close the calyx. Tackstitch the edges to the wrong side of the flower. Anchor knot the thread.

Tackstitch.

Finished flower

Pincushion Flower

Pincushion Flower with Pinch Tip Leaf-M (page 113). Use same ribbon width for both petals and leaf.

SKILL LEVEL: *Advanced* ◆◆◆

Suggested Ribbon

2 different colors and widths of woven ribbon with a soft or medium hand, double-sided

Amount Needed

- **Center:** Approximately 19 × width of Color 1 ribbon plus ½"*
- **Petals:** Approximately 72 × width of Color 2 ribbon plus ½"* (Use ribbon ⅛" narrower than Color 1.)

Additional Supplies

- 2RW circle of crinoline

Measure

Ribbon width (RW)	Center: Color 1	Ribbon width (RW)	Petals: Color 2
	Measure 1RW per petal.*		Measure 4RW per petal.*
1"	1"	¾"	3"
⅞"	⅞"	⅝"	2½"
¾"	¾"	½"	2"
⅝"	⅝"	⅜"	1½"
½"	½"	¼"	1"

* Do not cut the ribbon until instructed to do so.

DIRECTIONS

See General Directions (page 144), Crinkle Fold Petals (page 37), and Star Point Petals (page 33).

Pincushion Center

1. Follow Steps 1–3 for the Crinkle Fold Petals; pin 19 petals. Anchor knot the thread at the beginning of the first fold. Working from behind, take a whipstitch through each fold, back and forth in a zigzag pattern, through all the layers of ribbon.

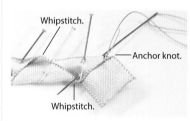

2. Follow Step 5, but allow the inner petals to rise. Anchor knot but do not cut the thread.

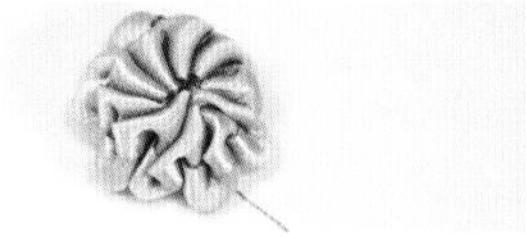

Finished center

Flower

1. Mark 18 Star Point Petals 4RW (see chart). Follow Star Point Petals through Step 2, gathering each petal tightly (see tip below). Follow Step 3, arranging the petals evenly and leaving a 1RW opening in the middle of the flower. Tackstitch the inner gathered edge to the crinoline, with the raw edges facing in. Anchor knot and cut the thread.

> **tip**
>
> It's easier to control the petals if you anchor knot the thread after every 4 or 5 petals.

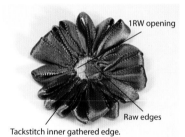

Tackstitch inner gathered edge.

2. Tackstitch the center into the middle of the flower. Anchor knot the thread.

Finished flower

BOHEMIAN FLOWERS

These blooms remind us of wooden caravans painted in colorful patterns, and doors decorated with bells hanging from satin ribbons. They are offered here for those who remember the old ways, with a free gypsy spirit and an artistic soul.

HIBISCUS ... 83
1½" silk bias ribbon with
Winged Leaf:
1" French wire ribbon

PASSION FLOWER ... 89
⅜" and ⅝" satin ribbon with
Art Nouveau Leaf-M:
⅝" satin ribbon

MOULIN ROUGE ... 84
2 colors of ⅜" satin ribbon with
Deco Leaf-L:
⅜" satin ribbon

BALLERINA FUCHSIA ... 90
2 colors of ⅝" satin ribbon with
Baroque Leaf:
⅝" French wire ribbon

GYPSY DANDELION ... 85
1" and ⅝" silk bias ribbon with
Oval Leaf-L:
1" silk bias ribbon

LILY OF THE VALLEY ... 91
⅝" satin ribbon with
Deco Leaf-S:
⅜" satin ribbon

PUCK'S ROSE ... 86
⅝" double-sided silk satin ribbon
with *Soft Curve Leaf:*
⅝" satin ribbon

COURT JESTER ... 92
2 colors of ⅜" satin ribbon with
Art Nouveau Leaf-M:
⅜" satin ribbon

SPANISH DANCER ... 87
⅜" and ⅝" satin ribbon with
Hooded Leaf-M:
⅝" satin ribbon

ROYAL DAHLIA ... 93
⅜" and ⅝" satin ribbon with
Neapolitan Leaf-S:
⅝" French wire ribbon

ORCHID ... 88
⅝" French wire ribbon and ⅝"
satin ribbon with *Slender Tip
Leaf-M:* ⅝" French wire ribbon

CLAIRE DE LUNE ... 94
2 colors of ⅝" satin ribbon with
Ruched Leaf:
⅜" satin ribbon

Hibiscus

Hibiscus with Winged Leaf (page 123). Use ribbon ½" narrower for leaf than for flower.

SKILL LEVEL: *Intermediate* ◆◆

Suggested Ribbon

Silk bias ribbon: habotai or satin

Amount Needed

▪ Approximately 15 × width of project ribbon plus ½"*

Additional Supplies

▪ 3" rayon cord

Measure

Ribbon width (RW)	Measure 3RW per petal.*
1½"	4½"
1"	3"
¾"	2¼"
⅝"	1⅞"
½"	1½"
⁷⁄₁₆"	1⁵⁄₁₆"

* Do not cut the ribbon until instructed to do so.

DIRECTIONS

See General Directions (page 144) and Gather and Grab Petals (page 30).

 note

Use the original width of the ribbon to calculate the RW measurements. Where the directions for the Gather and Grab Petals refer to the bias edge, that will be the folded edge of this flower; the folded edges will be the bias edge of this flower.

1. Gently pull out a single strand from the middle of the rayon cord to create a raveled edge.

Pull out 1 strand from center.

2. Fold and gently finger-press the width of the ribbon in half. Pin 5 Gather and Grab Petals 3RW (see chart), with the folded edge as the outer edge. Follow Steps 2 and 3 for Gather and Grab Petals, inserting the needle through both layers of ribbon at the folded edge.

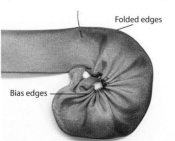

Folded edges

Bias edges

3. Follow the remaining directions through Step 5 to "Match the right sides of the raw edges."

4. Insert the rayon cord into the middle of the flower; adjust the length and trim as needed. Pull the thread tight. Tackstitch the rayon cord to the raw edges of the flower. Anchor knot the thread.

Tackstitch.

Finished flower

Moulin Rouge

Moulin Rouge with Deco Leaf-L (page 118). Use same ribbon width for both center and leaf.

SKILL LEVEL: **Advanced** ◆◆◆

Suggested Ribbon

2 different colors of woven ribbon with a soft or medium hand, single- or double-sided

Amount Needed

▪ **Petals:** Approximately 20 × combined width of Color 1 and Color 2 ribbons plus ½"* (Use ribbon in same width and length for Color 1 and Color 2.)

▪ **Center:** 8 × width of Color 1 ribbon

DIRECTIONS

See General Directions (page 144), Two-Color Ribbon (page 15), Gathered Loop Petals (page 35), and Ruffled Rosette (page 129).

 note

Use the combined width to calculate the RW measurements for the petals.

1. Using Colors 1 and 2, follow the directions for Two-Color Ribbon.

Petals: Pin 10 Gathered Loop Petals 2RW (see chart); follow Gathered Loop Petals through Step 4. Note: The ribbon on the right in Step 2 will be on the bottom edge of the flower.

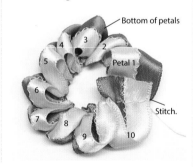

2. In Step 5, pull the thread tight, leaving a 1RW opening in the middle of the flower. Anchor knot and cut the thread.

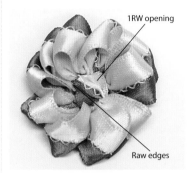

3. Center: Cut 1 length of ribbon 8RW from Color 1. Follow the directions for the Ruffled Rosette; do not cut the thread.

4. Flower: Tackstitch the center into the middle of the petals. Anchor knot the thread.

Measure and Cut

Original ribbon width (RW)	Combined width	Petals: Color 1 and Color 2	Ribbon width (RW)	Center: Color 1
		Measure 2RW per petal.*		Cut 1 length 8RW.
⅝"	1¼"	2½"	⅝"	5"
½"	1"	2"	½"	4"
⅜"	¾"	1½"	⅜"	3"
¼"	½"	1"	¼"	2"

* Do not cut the ribbon until instructed to do so.

Finished flower

Gypsy Dandelion

Gypsy Dandelion with Oval Leaf-L (page 120). Use same ribbon width for both outer layer and leaf.

SKILL LEVEL: **Intermediate** ◆◆

Suggested Ribbon

2 different colors and widths of silk bias habotai ribbon

Amount Needed

- ▪ **Outer layer:** 12 × width of Color 1 ribbon
- ▪ **Center:** 4 × width of Color 2 ribbon (Use ribbon approximately ½" narrower than Color 1.)

Additional Supplies

- ▪ Small amount of stuffing
- ▪ Second threaded needle

DIRECTIONS

See General Directions (page 144), Double Daisy (page 69), and Berry and Stuffed Berry (page 131).

 note

Use the original width of the ribbon to calculate the RW measurements.

1. Outer layer: Cut 1 length of ribbon 12RW (see chart). Follow Steps 1 and 2 for the Double Daisy.

2. Beginning next to the seam and stitching through both layers of ribbon, follow the directions for the outer edge detail stitch (page 143). Pull the gathers in gently.

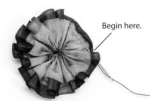

Begin here.

3. Center: Cut 1 length of ribbon 4RW (see chart). Using the second needle, follow the directions for the Stuffed Berry. Tackstitch the center into the middle of the outer layer. Anchor knot and cut the thread.

4. Pull the gathers of the first needle to form the outer layer around the center. Tackstitch and anchor knot the thread.

Tackstitch.

Finished flower

Measure and Cut

Ribbon width (RW)	Outer layer: Color 1	Ribbon width (RW)	Center: Color 2
	Cut 1 length 12RW.		Cut 1 length 4RW.
1½"	18"	1"	4"
1"	12"	⅝"	2½"
¾"	9"	⁷⁄₁₆"	1¾"

Puck's Rose

Puck's Rose with Soft Curve Leaf (page 111). Use same ribbon width for both flower and leaf.

SKILL LEVEL: *Intermediate* ◆◆

Suggested Ribbon

Woven or French wire ribbon with a soft, medium, or stiff hand, double-sided

Amount Needed

▪ Approximately 8 × width of project ribbon plus 1"*

* Do not cut the ribbon until instructed to do so.

DIRECTIONS

See General Directions (page 144).

1. Center petal: Fold the ribbon over and down at a 90° angle, leaving a ½" tail of ribbon below the selvage edge. Anchor knot the thread at the fold next to the selvage edge. Roll the folded edge toward the perpendicular selvage edge. Tackstitch through the folds and horizontal selvage edge.

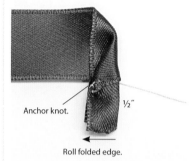

Anchor knot. ½"

Roll folded edge.

2. Petals: Fold the ribbon behind and down at a 90° angle and repeat Step 1.

Tackstitch. Roll.

3. Repeat Step 2 for 5 more petals.

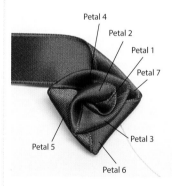

Petal 4
Petal 2
Petal 1
Petal 7
Petal 3
Petal 6
Petal 5

4. Measure 1RW plus ½"; cut the ribbon. Fold the raw edge down to the beginning raw edge. Anchor knot the thread.

5. Beginning at the last petal, insert the needle through the corner of the petal using a whip-stitch. Take 1 tack stitch through the raw edges. Pull the thread slightly to curve the petal.

Last petal   Whipstitch.

Tackstitch.

6. Repeat for each of the 4 outer petals. Anchor knot the thread.

Outer petals

Finished flower

Spanish Dancer

Spanish Dancer with Hooded Leaf-M (page 123). Use same ribbon width for both outer petals and leaf.

SKILL LEVEL: *Intermediate* ◆◆

Suggested Ribbon

2 colors and widths of woven ribbon with a soft or medium hand, single- or double-sided

Amount Needed

■ **Center:** 16 × width of Color 1 ribbon

■ **Outer layer:** 16 × width of Color 2 ribbon (Use ribbon ¼" wider than Color 1.)

■ **Outer layer:** Color 1 ribbon in same length as Color 2

Additional Supplies

■ 2RW crinoline circle

Measure and Cut

Ribbon width (RW)	Center: Color 1	Ribbon width (RW)	Outer layer: Color 2
	Cut 1 length 16RW.		Cut 1 length 16RW.
¾"	12"	1"	16"
⅝"	10"	⅞"	14"
½"	8"	¾"	12"
⅜"	6"	⅝"	10"
¼"	4"	½"	8"

DIRECTIONS

See General Directions (page 144), Double Posy (page 28), Inner Edge Layering (page 16), and Rosette (page 25).

1. Center: Cut 1 length of ribbon 16RW (see chart) from Color 1. Follow the directions for the Double Posy. Tackstitch the middle of the center to the crinoline. Anchor knot and cut the thread.

Tackstitch.

2. Outer layer: Cut 1 length of ribbon 16RW (see chart) from Color 2. Follow the directions for inner edge layering using Color 1. Follow the directions for the Rosette through Step 2, stitching through 2 layers; gently pull the thread to form the middle of the flower.

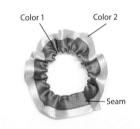

Color 1   Color 2

Seam

3. Insert the center into the middle of the outer layer; pull the thread tight. Tackstitch the inner gathers to the crinoline. Anchor knot the thread.

Tackstitch.

Finished flower

Orchid

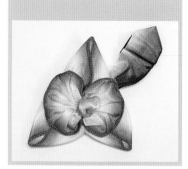

Orchid with Slender Tip Leaf-M (page 115). Use same ribbon width for both leaf and petals.

SKILL LEVEL: **Intermediate** ◆◆

Suggested Ribbon

2 different colors of woven or French wire ribbon with a soft or medium hand, single- or double-sided

Amount Needed

▪ **Center:** 6 × width of Color 1 ribbon

▪ **Petals:** Approximately 20 × width of Color 2 ribbon plus ½"*

DIRECTIONS

See General Directions (page 144), Single or Double Knot (page 128), Boat Gather Petals (page 29), Soft Curve Leaf or Petal (page 111), and Simple Flower (page 116).

1. Center: Cut 1 length of ribbon 6RW (see chart). Follow the directions for the Single Knot.

Inner petals: Mark 2 Boat Gather Petals 4RW. Follow Boat Gather Petals through Step 4 to "Match the right sides of the raw edges."

2. Insert the Single Knot into the middle of the inner petals. Pull the thread tight. Tackstitch, anchor knot, and cut the thread.

3. Outer petals: Cut 3 lengths of ribbon 4RW. Follow the directions for the Soft Curve Petal for each length. Follow Steps 2 and 3 for the Simple Flower.

4. Flower: Insert the inner petals into the middle of the outer petals, arranging the petals evenly. Pull the thread tight and tackstitch the raw edges together. Anchor knot the thread.

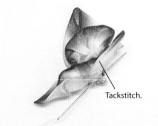

Tackstitch.

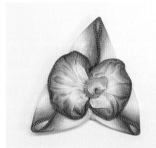

Finished flower

Measure and Cut

Ribbon width (RW)	Center: Color 1	Inner petals: Color 2	Outer petals: Color 2
	Cut 1 length 6RW.	Measure 4RW per petal.*	Cut 3 lengths 4RW.
1"	6"	4"	4"
⅞"	5¼"	3½"	3½"
¾"	4½"	3"	3"
⅝"	3¾"	2½"	2½"
½"	3"	2"	2"
⅜"	2¼"	1½"	1½"

* Do not cut the ribbon until instructed to do so.

Passion Flower

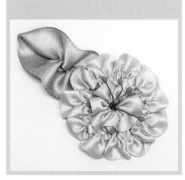

Passion Flower with Art Nouveau Leaf-M (page 119). Use ribbon ¼″ wider for leaf than for petals.

SKILL LEVEL: *Advanced* ◆◆◆

Suggested Ribbon

2 different colors and widths of woven ribbon with a soft or medium hand, single- or double-sided

Amount Needed

- **Center:** 8 × width of Color 1 ribbon
- **Center:** Color 2 ribbon (Use ribbon ¼″ narrower than Color 1 in same length.)
- **Petals:** 43 × width of Color 2 ribbon plus ½″* (Use ribbon ¼″ narrower than Color 1.)

Additional Supplies

- 4RW circle of crinoline
- 3 folded stamens

Measure and Cut

Ribbon width (RW)	Center: Color 1	Ribbon width (RW)	Center: Color 2	Petals: Color 2	
	Cut 1 length 8RW.		Cut 1 length same as Color 1.	Measure 3RW per petal.*	Measure 1RW per petal.*
1″	8″	¾″	8″	2¼″	¾″
⅞″	7″	⅝″	7″	1⅞″	⅝″
¾″	6″	½″	6″	1½″	½″
⅝″	5″	⅜″	5″	1⅛″	⅜″
½″	4″	¼″	4″	¾″	¼″

* Do not cut the ribbon until instructed to do so.

DIRECTIONS

See General Directions (page 144), Double Rosette (page 129), and Gala Gather Petals (page 31).

1. Center: Cut 1 length of each ribbon 8RW of the wider ribbon (see chart). Follow the directions for the Double Rosette, adding the stamens before pulling up the gathers. Tackstitch the middle and outer edges of the center to the crinoline. Anchor knot and cut the thread.

2. Petals: Mark 21 Gala Gather Petals, alternating between 3RW and 1RW lengths (see chart). Follow Gala Gather Petals through Step 4 to "Match the right sides of the raw edges."

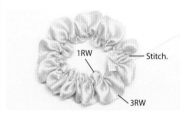

3. Insert the center into the middle of the petals. Pull the thread tightly, allowing the inner petals to rest gently around the center. Tackstitch the inner lobes to the crinoline. Anchor knot the thread.

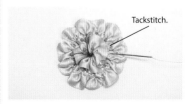

Finished flower

Ballerina Fuchsia

Ballerina Fuchsia with Baroque Leaf (page 122). Use same ribbon width for both flower and leaf.

SKILL LEVEL: *Advanced* ◆◆◆

Suggested Ribbon

2 different colors of woven ribbon with a soft or medium hand, single- or double-sided

Amount Needed

▪ **Inner petals:** 16 × width of Color 1 ribbon

▪ **Outer petals and bulb:** Approximately 18 × width of Color 2 ribbon plus ½"*

Additional Supplies

▪ 3 folded stamens

Measure and Cut

Ribbon width (RW)	Inner petals: Color 1	Outer petals: Color 2	Bulb: Color 2
	Cut 4 lengths 4RW.	Measure 3RW per petal.*	Cut 1 length 6RW.
1"	4"	3"	6"
⅞"	3½"	2⅝"	5¼"
¾"	3"	2¼"	4½"
⅝"	2½"	1⅞"	3¾"
½"	2"	1½"	3"
⅜"	1½"	1⅛"	2¼"

* Do not cut the ribbon until instructed to do so.

DIRECTIONS

See General Directions (page 144), Miter Fold Leaf or Petal (page 115), Simple Flower (page 116), Boat Gather Petals (page 29), and Berry and Stuffed Berry (page 131).

1. Inner petals: Cut 4 lengths of ribbon 4RW (see chart). Follow the directions for the Miter Fold Petal for each length; cut the thread. Follow Step 2 of the Simple Flower, with the right side of the petals facing out.

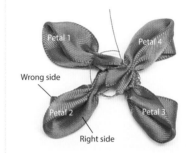

Petal 1 Petal 4
Wrong side
Petal 2 Petal 3
Right side

2. Follow Steps 3 and 4 of the Simple Flower, inserting the stamens into the middle of the inner petals in Step 3. Anchor knot and cut the thread.

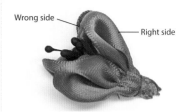

Wrong side   Right side

3. Outer petals: Mark 4 Boat Gather Petals 3RW (see chart). Follow Boat Gather Petals through Step 4 to "Match the right sides of the raw edges." Allow the raw edges to face up.

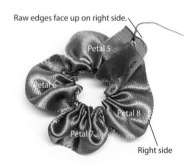

Raw edges face up on right side.
Petal 5
Petal 6
Petal 8
Petal 7
Right side

4. Insert the raw edges of the inner petals through the wrong side of the opening. Align the stitching of each inner petal with the gathered portion of the outer petals. Tackstitch, anchor knot, and cut the thread.

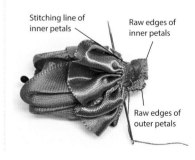

Stitching line of inner petals   Raw edges of inner petals
Raw edges of outer petals

5. Bulb: Cut 1 length of ribbon 6RW (see chart). Follow Steps 1 and 2 for the Berry, but allow the gathered portion to form on the right side of the ribbon as for the Rosette.

6. Insert the raw edges of the flower into the opening of the bulb. Gently pull in the gathers to close the bulb; tackstitch. Whipstitch the edges of the bulb to the gathered edges of the outer petals. Anchor knot the thread.

Bulb

Whipstitch.

Outer petals

Finished flower

Lily of the Valley

Lily of the Valley with Deco Leaf-S (page 118). Use ribbon ¼" narrower for leaf than for flower.

SKILL LEVEL: **Easy** ◆

Suggested Ribbon

Woven or French wire ribbon with a soft or medium hand, single- or double-sided

Amount Needed

▪ 18 × width of project ribbon

Additional Supplies

▪ Wire stem (page 126): 1
▪ Wire tendril (page 126): 3
▪ Deco Leaf (page 118): 3

DIRECTIONS

1. Cut 1 length of ribbon 6RW; see Ballerina Fuchsia (page 90) for cutting chart and references. Follow Steps 1–3 for the Berry (page 131), but allow the gathered portion to form on the right side of the ribbon as for the Rosette (page 25). Cut 2 more lengths; repeat for each length.

Finished flower

2. Tackstitch a leaf to the top edge of a flower. Glue the wrong side of the leaf to the wire stem. Glue a wire tendril close to the flower. Repeat for the remaining components.

Flower with leaf and tendril

Court Jester

Court Jester with Art Nouveau Leaf-M
(page 119). Use same width for leaf as
for flower.

SKILL LEVEL: *Intermediate* ◆◆

Suggested Ribbon

2 different colors of woven ribbon
with a soft or medium hand,
double-sided

Amount Needed

▪ **Outer petals:** Approximately
23 × width of Color 1 ribbon
plus ½"*

▪ **Center:** Approximately
19 × width of Color 2 ribbon
plus ½"*

Additional Supplies

▪ 3RW crinoline circle

Measure

Ribbon width (RW)	Outer petals: Color 1	Center: Color 2
	Measure 3RW per petal.*	Measure 1RW per petal.*
1"	3"	1"
⅞"	2⅝"	⅞"
¾"	2¼"	¾"
⅝"	1⅞"	⅝"
½"	1½"	½"
⅜"	1⅛"	⅜"

* Do not cut the ribbon until instructed to do so.

DIRECTIONS

*See General Directions (page 144),
Pincushion Center (page 80), and
Folded Petals (page 34).*

1. **Outer petals:** Pin 6 Folded
Petals 3RW (see chart). Follow the
remaining directions for Folded
Petals through Step 4 to "Match
the right sides of the raw edges."

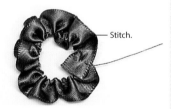

Stitch.

2. Tackstitch the gathered edge
to the crinoline circle, leaving a
2RW opening in the middle of the
flower. Anchor knot and cut the
thread.

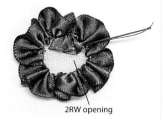

2RW opening

3. **Center:** Follow the directions for the Pincushion Center,
stitching 19 petals. Slightly pull in
the gathers to allow the petals to
lie flat.

4. **Flower:** Tackstitch the inner
lobes of the center to the crinoline. Anchor knot the thread.

Tackstitch.

Finished flower

Royal Dahlia

Royal Dahlia with Neapolitan Leaf-S (page 118). Use same ribbon width for leaf as wider ribbon for flower.

SKILL LEVEL: *Advanced* ◆◆◆

Suggested Ribbon

2 different colors and widths of woven ribbon with a soft or medium hand, single- or double-sided

Amount Needed

▪ **Petals and center:**
32 × combined width of project ribbon (Use 2 different flower-colored ribbons in the same length, with 1 of them ¼" narrower than the other.)

DIRECTIONS

See General Directions (page 144), Two-Color Ribbon (page 15), Prairie Point Leaf or Petal (page 111), Simple Flower (page 116), and Rose Hips (page 130).

 note

Use the combined width to calculate the RW measurements.

1. Follow the directions for Two-Color Ribbon.

Petals: Cut 8 lengths of ribbon 3RW (see chart). Follow the directions for the Prairie Point Petal for each length, with the folded edges facing forward and the wider ribbon on the bottom. Trim the raw edges down to ¼".

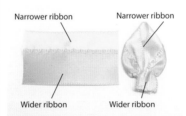

Narrower ribbon   Narrower ribbon

Wider ribbon   Wider ribbon

2. Follow Steps 2 and 5 for the Simple Flower. Anchor knot and cut the thread.

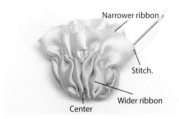

3. Center: Cut 1 length of ribbon 8RW (see chart). Follow the directions for Rose Hips, stitching the wider ribbon as the middle of the center. Stitch the needle down through the middle of the center to the gathered edges.

Narrower ribbon

Stitch.

Wider ribbon

Center

4. Flower: Tackstitch the center to the middle of the petals. Anchor knot the thread.

Finished flower

Measure and Cut

Original ribbon width (RW)	Combined width	Cut 8 lengths 3RW.	Cut 1 length 8RW.
¾" and ½"	1¼"	3¾"	10"
⅝" and ⅜"	1"	3"	8"
½" and ¼"	¾"	2¼"	6"
⅜" and ⅛"	½"	1½"	4"

Claire de Lune

Claire de Lune with Ruched Leaf (page 119). Use ribbon ¼" narrower for leaf than for petals.

SKILL LEVEL: *Easy* ◊

Suggested Ribbon

2 different colors of woven ribbon with a soft or medium hand, single- or double-sided

Amount Needed

- **Center:** 6 × width of Color 1 ribbon
- **Petals:** Approximately 28 × width of Color 2 ribbon plus ½"*

Additional Supplies

- 2RW crinoline circle

Measure and Cut

Ribbon width (RW)	Center: Color 1	Petals: Color 2	
	Cut 1 length 6RW.	Measure 3RW per petal.*	Measure 2RW per petal.*
1"	6"	3"	2"
⅞"	5¼"	2⅝"	1¾"
¾"	4½"	2¼"	1½"
⅝"	3¾"	1⅞"	1¼"
½"	3"	1½"	1"
⅜"	2¼"	1⅛"	¾"

* Do not cut the ribbon until instructed to do so.

DIRECTIONS

See General Directions (page 144), Jelly Roll Center (page 128), and Gala Gather Petals (page 31).

1. Center: Cut 1 length of ribbon 6RW (see chart). Follow the directions for the Jelly Roll Center. Tackstitch the bottom edge of the center into the middle of the crinoline. Anchor knot and cut the thread.

2. Petals: Mark 11 Gala Gather Petals in this pattern: 3RW and 2RW lengths (see chart). Follow Gala Gather Petals through Step 4 to "Match the right sides of the raw edges."

3. Flower: Insert the center through the middle of the petals. Pull the thread tightly, arranging the 2RW petals facing upward around the center, and the 3RW petals flat against the crinoline. Tackstitch the gathered middle of the petals to the crinoline. Anchor knot the thread.

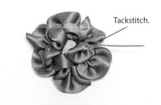

Tackstitch.

Finished flower

ELEGANT FLOWERS

Well-tended rose beds and stately garden walks are filled with these gentle, elegant, and luscious blooms. Imagine a grand porcelain vase or simple mason jar overflowing with these lovely, precious blossoms.

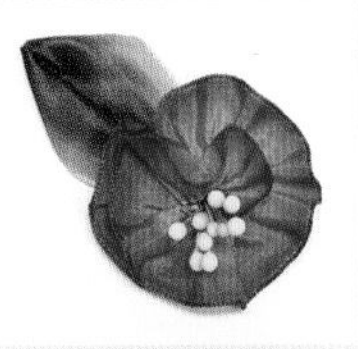

GENTLE LADY ... 97
⅝" French wire ribbon with
Deco Leaf-M:
⅝" French wire ribbon

ENGLISH MISS ... 98
1" silk bias ribbon with
Oval Leaf-S:
1" silk bias ribbon

PETITE BUD ... 99
⅞" satin ribbon

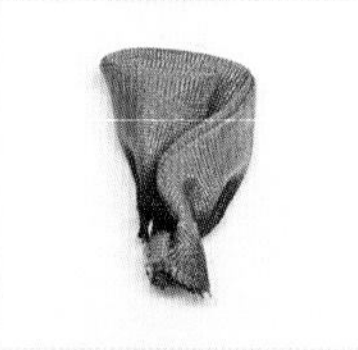

SILK BLOOM ... 99
1" silk bias ribbon

CHOU ROSE ... 100
⅝" silk satin ribbon with
Sweet Leaf-S:
⅝" taffeta ribbon

FONTANA ROSE ... 101
⅜" satin ribbon with
Neapolitan Leaf-L:
⅜" satin ribbon

SAUCY MISS ... 102
1" silk bias ribbon with
Frilly Leaf-S:
1" silk bias ribbon

POMPOM ROSE ...103
⅜" and ⅝" satin ribbon with
Deco Leaf-S:
⅝" satin ribbon

SYMPHONY ROSE ... 104
½" satin ribbon with
Sweet Leaf-M:
⅝" satin ribbon

GUINEVERE'S ROSE ... 105
1" silk bias ribbon with
Renaissance Leaf-M:
1" silk bias ribbon

VINTAGE FAVORITE ... 106
⅜" satin ribbon with
Neapolitan Leaf-M:
⅜" satin ribbon

ROMANTIC ROSE ... 108
⅜" satin ribbon with
Art Nouveau Leaf-M:
⅜" satin ribbon

Gentle Lady

Gentle Lady with Deco Leaf-M (page 118). Use same ribbon width for both flower and leaf.

SKILL LEVEL: **Easy** ◆

Suggested Ribbon

Woven or French wire ribbon with a soft or medium hand, single- or double-sided

Amount Needed

▦ 18 × width of project ribbon

Additional Supplies

▦ 2RW crinoline circle

▦ 5 folded stamens

▦ Second threaded needle

Measure and Cut

Ribbon width (RW)	Cut 1 length 18RW.
1″	18″
⅞″	15¾″
¾″	13½″
⅝″	11¼″
½″	9″
⅜″	6¾″

DIRECTIONS

See General Directions (page 144) and Posy (page 26).

1. Clip a small hole through the center of the crinoline. Insert the folded stamens through the hole. Tackstitch to the wrong side of the crinoline with the second needle.

2. Cut 1 length of ribbon 18RW (see chart). Follow the directions for the Posy through Step 2. Gently pull the thread to form the middle of the flower.

3. Curve the beginning edge around the stamens. With the second needle, tackstitch the beginning raw edge to the crinoline.

Tackstitch.

Second needle

4. Spiral the length around the center counterclockwise. Tackstitch the inner gathered edges to the crinoline as you spiral, adjusting the gathers evenly or loosening them as you reach the outer edges of the flower.

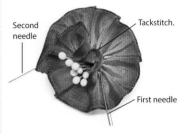

Second needle

Tackstitch.

First needle

5. Trim the crinoline. Tuck the last raw edge next to the crinoline. Anchor knot and cut the first thread. Tackstitch and anchor knot the second thread.

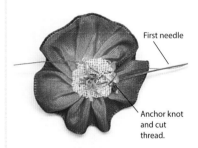

First needle

Anchor knot and cut thread.

Finished flower

English Miss

English Miss with Oval Leaf-S (page 120). Use same ribbon width for both flower and leaf.

SKILL LEVEL: *Intermediate* ◆◆

Suggested Ribbon

Silk bias ribbon: habotai, satin, or velvet

Amount Needed

- Small flower:

6 × width of project ribbon

- Medium flower:

12 × width of project ribbon

- Large flower:

18 × width of project ribbon

Additional Supplies

- Small flower:

½RW crinoline circle

- Medium flower:

1RW crinoline circle

- Large flower:

1½RW crinoline circle

- Second threaded needle

Measure and Cut

Ribbon width (RW)	Small flower	Medium flower	Large flower
	Cut 1 length 6RW.	Cut 1 length 12RW.	Cut 1 length 18RW.
1"	6"	12"	18"
¾"	4½"	9"	13½
⅝"	3¾"	7½"	11¼
½"	3"	6"	9"
⁷⁄₁₆"	2⅝"	5¼"	7⅞"

DIRECTIONS

See General Directions (page 144), Posy (page 26), and Gentle Lady (page 97).

 note

Use the original width of the ribbon to calculate the RW measurements. Where the directions for the Posy refer to the outer selvage edge, that will be the folded edge of this flower. The inner selvage edge will be the bias edges of this flower.

1. Cut 1 length of ribbon (see chart). Fold and gently finger-press the width of the ribbon in half. Follow the directions for the Posy through Step 2. Gently pull the thread to form the middle of the flower.

2. With the second needle, tack-stitch the beginning raw edge to the center of the crinoline.

Second needle

Raw edges

3. Follow Steps 4 and 5 for the Gentle Lady.

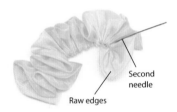

Tackstitch.

Large

Medium

Small

Finished flowers

Petite Bud

Petite Bud

Suggested Ribbon

Woven ribbon with a soft or medium hand, single- or double-sided

Amount Needed
- 6RW

DIRECTIONS

See General Directions (page 144) and Double Posy (page 28).

1. Cut 1 length of ribbon 6RW. Fold the length of ribbon in half. Follow Steps 1 and 2 for the Double Posy, marking ½RW from the raw edges.

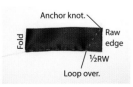

Anchor knot.
Fold
Raw edge
½RW
Loop over.

2. Pull in the gathers tightly. Anchor knot the thread at the fold.

3. Roll the ribbon upon itself, beginning with the folded edge to the inside and finishing with the curved edge on the outside. Tackstitch the gathered selvage edges together. Anchor knot the thread.

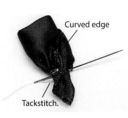

Curved edge
Tackstitch.

Finished bud

Silk Bloom

Silk Bloom

Suggested Ribbon

Silk bias ribbon: habotai, satin, or velvet

Amount Needed
- 3RW

DIRECTIONS

See General Directions (page 144), Double Posy (page 28), and Petite Bud (at left).

> *note*
>
> *Use the original width of the ribbon to calculate the ribbon width (RW) measurements.*

1. Cut 1 length of ribbon 3RW. Fold the width of ribbon in half; fold the length of ribbon in half. Follow Steps 1 and 2 for the Double Posy, marking ½RW from the raw edges.

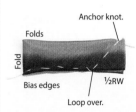

Anchor knot.
Folds
Fold
Bias edges
½RW
Loop over.

2. Follow Steps 2 and 3 for the Petite Bud.

Finished bud

Use the Ribbon Cutting Chart (page 146) to find the correct RW measurement for the Petite Bud and Silk Bloom.

Chou Rose

Chou Rose with Sweet Leaf-S (page 117). Use same ribbon width for both flower and leaf.

SKILL LEVEL: **Advanced** ◆◆◆

Suggested Ribbon

Woven ribbon with a soft or medium hand, double-sided

Amount Needed

- Approximately 16 × width of project ribbon*

Do not cut the ribbon until instructed to do so.

Additional Supplies

- 2RW crinoline circle

DIRECTIONS

See General Directions (page 144).

1. Fold the raw edge under 1RW. Beginning at the top left edge of the fold, whipstitch the 4 corners counterclockwise, ending at the top right edge. This is the center of the flower.

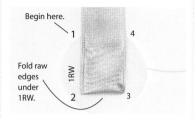

Begin here.
1   4
Fold raw edges under 1RW.
1RW
2   3

2. Fold the length of the ribbon toward you; then fold it down and to the left at a bias angle. Tackstitch the left corner edge of the ribbon to the crinoline circle. This is the first petal.

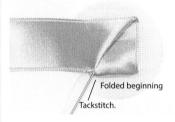

Folded beginning
Tackstitch.

3. Rotate the circle clockwise ¼ turn. Tackstitch the ribbon to the crinoline at the right corner edge.

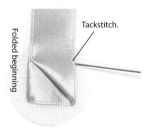

Folded beginning
Tackstitch.

4. Repeat Steps 2 and 3 as many times as needed, working your way to the outer edges of the crinoline circle. At this point, you can trim the crinoline smaller if needed.

5. Stitch the last petal; trim off the excess crinoline. Tackstitch the corners of the outer petals to the crinoline a second time. Cut off the length of ribbon, leaving a ½" tail.

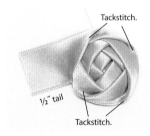

Tackstitch.
½" tail
Tackstitch.

6. Fold the raw edge over to the wrong side of the crinoline circle. Gather stitch across the width of the tail, just below the crinoline. Tackstitch to the crinoline. Anchor knot the thread.

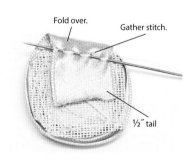

Fold over.
Gather stitch.
½" tail

Finished flower

Fontana Rose

Fontana Rose with Neapolitan Leaf-L (page 118). Use same ribbon width for both flower and leaf.

SKILL LEVEL: **Intermediate** ◆◆

Suggested Ribbon

Woven or French wire ribbon with a soft or medium hand, double-sided

Amount Needed

▪ Approximately 59 × width of project ribbon plus ½"*

Additional Supplies

▪ 4RW crinoline circle

▪ 5 folded stamens

▪ Second threaded needle

Measure

Ribbon width (RW)	Measure 3RW per petal.*
1"	3"
⅞"	2⅝"
¾"	2¼"
⅝"	1⅞"
½"	1½"
⅜"	1⅛"

* Do not cut the ribbon until instructed to do so.

DIRECTIONS

See General Directions (page 144), Gentle Lady (page 97), and Folded Petals (page 34).

1. Follow Step 1 for the Gentle Lady.

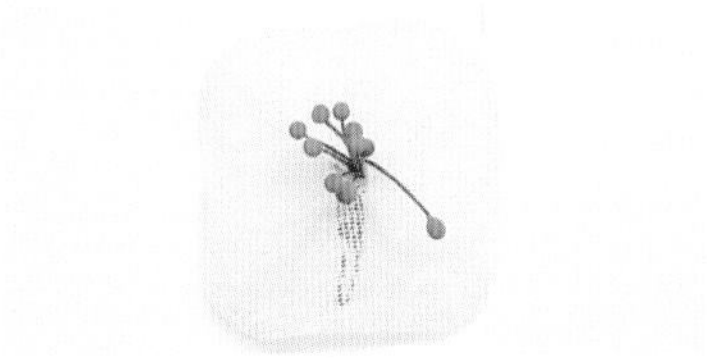

2. Pin 15 Folded Petals 3RW (see chart). Follow Folded Petals through Step 3. Gently pull the thread to form the petals and the middle of the flower.

3. Curve the beginning edge around the stamens. With the second needle, tackstitch the beginning raw edge to the crinoline.

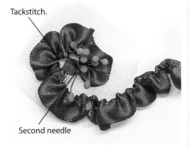

Tackstitch.

Second needle

4. Follow Steps 4 and 5 for the Gentle Lady. Tackstitch the inner gathered edges to the crinoline as you spiral the length counterclockwise around the center, relaxing the gathers of the outer petals of the rose.

Finished flower

Elegant Fontana Rose Purse, 4" × 5"

Saucy Miss

Saucy Miss with Frilly Leaf-S (page 121).
Use same ribbon width for both flower
and leaf.

SKILL LEVEL: *Intermediate* ◆◆

Suggested Ribbon

Silk bias habotai ribbon

Amount Needed

▪ 24 × width of project ribbon

Additional Supplies

▪ 1.5RW crinoline circle

▪ 5 folded stamens

▪ Second threaded needle

Measure and Cut

Ribbon width (RW)	Cut 1 length 24RW.
1"	24"
¾"	18"
⅝"	15"
½"	12"

DIRECTIONS

See General Directions (page 144),
Gentle Lady (page 97), and Posy
(page 26).

 note

*Use the original width of the
ribbon to calculate the RW
measurements. Where the
directions for the Posy refer
to the outer selvage edge,
that will be the bias edges of
this flower; the inner selvage
edge will be the folded edge
of this flower.*

1. Follow Step 1 for the Gentle
Lady.

2. Cut 1 length of ribbon 24RW
(see chart). Fold and gently finger-
press the width of the ribbon to
⅝ the original width. Follow the
directions for the Posy through
Step 2. Gently pull the thread to
form the middle of the flower.

3. Curve the beginning edge
around the stamens. Tackstitch
the raw edge to the crinoline with
the second needle.

Tackstitch with
second needle.

4. Follow Steps 4 and 5 for the
Gentle Lady, spiraling the length
counterclockwise around the
center.

Tackstitch.

Finished flower

5. Detail edge option: Beginning
at the middle of the flower, using
the remaining needle, stitch
through both layers of ribbon.
Follow the directions for the outer
edge detail stitch (page 143) to the
end of the flower. Anchor knot
the thread.

Finished flower with outer edge detail

Pompom Rose

Pompom Rose with Deco Leaf-S (page 118). Use ribbon ¼″ wider for leaf than for outer layer.

SKILL LEVEL: *Intermediate* ◆ ◆

Suggested Ribbon

2 different colors and widths of woven ribbon with a soft or medium hand, single- or double-sided

Amount Needed

▪ **Outer layer:** 18 × width of Color 1 ribbon

▪ **Inner layer:** Color 2 ribbon (Use ribbon ¼″ narrower than Color 1 in same length.)

▪ **Center:** Approximately 32 × width of Color 2 ribbon plus ½″* (Use ribbon ¼″ narrower than Color 1.)

Additional Supplies

▪ 2RW crinoline circle

Measure and Cut

Ribbon width (RW)	Outer layer: Color 1	Ribbon width (RW)	Center: Color 2
	Cut 1 length 18RW.		Measure 1RW per petal.*
1″	18″	¾″	¾″
⅞″	15¾″	⅝″	⅝″
¾″	13½″	½″	½″
⅝″	11¼″	⅜″	⅜″
½″	9″	¼″	¼″

* Do not cut the ribbon until instructed to do so.

DIRECTIONS

See General Directions (page 144), Inner Edge Layering (page 16), Rosette (page 25), and Pouf Gather Center (page 132).

1. Outer layer / inner layer: Cut 1 length of ribbon 18RW (see chart) from Color 1. Using Color 2, follow the directions for inner edge layering. Follow the directions for the Rosette through Step 2, stitching through both layers. Gently pull the thread to gather the ribbon.

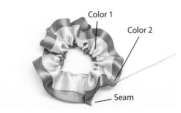

2. Tackstitch the gathered edges to the crinoline, leaving a 1RW opening in the middle of the flower. Anchor knot and cut the thread.

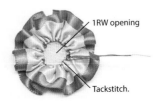

3. Center: Mark 16 Pouf Gathers. Follow the directions for the Pouf Gather Center.

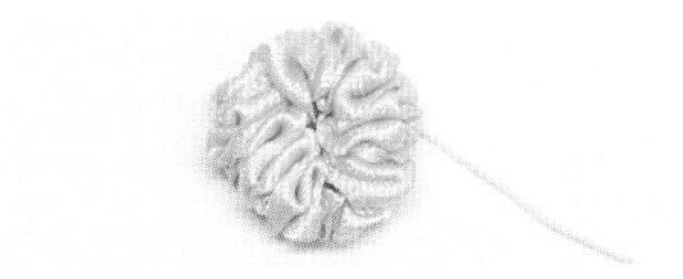

4. Flower: Tackstitch the center into the middle of the crinoline. Anchor knot the thread.

Finished flower

Symphony Rose

Symphony Rose with Sweet Leaf-S (page 117). Use ribbon ⅛″ wider for leaf than for flower.

SKILL LEVEL: **Intermediate** ◆◆

Suggested Ribbon

Woven or French wire ribbon with a soft or medium hand, double-sided

Amount Needed

▪ Approximately 20 × width of project ribbon plus ½″*

Do not cut the ribbon until instructed to do so.

Additional Supplies

▪ 2RW crinoline circle

▪ Second threaded needle

DIRECTIONS

See General Directions (page 144), Flip 'n Fold Petals (page 38), and Gentle Lady (page 97).

1. Follow the directions for Flip 'n Fold Petals through Step 3. Stitch 19 petals. Gently pull the thread to form the petals and the middle of the flower.

2. With the second needle, tackstitch the beginning raw edge to the center of the crinoline.

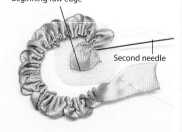

Beginning raw edge

Second needle

3. Continue to spiral the length counterclockwise around the center of the flower, tackstitching the inner gathered edges to the crinoline as you spiral. Follow Steps 4 and 5 for the Gentle Lady.

Finished flower

Symphony Rose Corsage, 4½″ × 2″

Guinevere's Rose

Guinevere's Rose with Renaissance Leaf-M (page 117). Use same ribbon width for both flower and leaf.

SKILL LEVEL: *Intermediate* ◆◆

Suggested Ribbon

Silk bias ribbon: habotai or satin

Amount Needed

▪ Approximately 24 × width of project ribbon*

Additional Supplies

▪ 1.5RW crinoline circle
▪ Second threaded needle

 note

Use the original width of the ribbon to calculate the RW measurements. Where the directions for the Gather and Grab Petals refer to the bias edges, that will be the folded edge of this flower; the folded edge of the Gather and Grab Petals will be the bias edges of this flower.

Measure

Ribbon width (RW)	Measure 1RW per petal.*	Measure 2RW per petal.*	Measure 3RW per petal.*
1″	1″	2″	3″
¾″	¾″	1½″	2¼″
⅝″	⅝″	1¼″	1⅞″
½″	½″	1″	1½″

* Do not cut the ribbon until instructed to do so.

DIRECTIONS

See General Directions (page 144), Gather and Grab Petals (page 30), and Gentle Lady (page 97).

1. Fold and gently finger-press the width of the ribbon in half. Pin the Gather and Grab Petals in this pattern: 4, 1RW; 4, 2RW; and 4, 3RW (see chart). Follow Gather and Grab Petals through Step 4.

2. With the second needle, tackstitch the beginning raw edge to the center of the crinoline. Tackstitch the first group of 4 petals into a circle.

3. Repeat Step 2 (below left) for the next group of 4 petals, spiraling the length counter-clockwise around the center group.

4. Follow Step 2 at left for the remaining group of petals. Follow Step 5 for the Gentle Lady.

Tackstitch.

Finished flower

Vintage Favorite

Vintage Favorite with Neapolitan Leaf-M (page 118). Use same ribbon width for both flower and leaf.

SKILL LEVEL: **Intermediate** ◆◆

Suggested Ribbon

Woven ribbon with a soft or medium hand, double-sided

Amount Needed

▪ Approximately 75 × width of project ribbon plus 2″

Additional Supplies

▪ 4RW crinoline circle

▪ Cotton darner threaded with perle cotton #8 in color that matches ribbon; knot tail

▪ Tapestry needle

▪ Threaded needle

Measure and Cut

Ribbon width (RW)	Cut 1 length 75RW plus 2″.
1″	77″
⅞″	67⅝″
¾″	58¼″
⅝″	48⅞″
½″	39½″
⅜″	30⅛″
¼″	20¾″
⅛″	11⅜″

DIRECTIONS

See General Directions (page 144).

1. Stitch the needle threaded with perle cotton through the center of the crinoline. Loop the thread over the edge and back through the center of the crinoline. This is 1 spoke. Stitch 3 more spokes around the crinoline as shown.

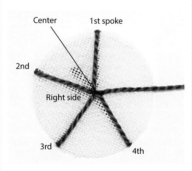

2. Loop the thread over the crinoline to form the last spoke. Anchor knot the perle cotton on the wrong side; cut the thread.

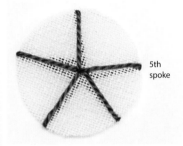

3. Cut 1 length of ribbon 75RW plus 2″ (see chart). Fold the raw edge of an end under 1RW; place over the center of the spokes, working on the right side. Tackstitch the 4 edges to the crinoline with the threaded needle. Anchor knot and cut the thread.

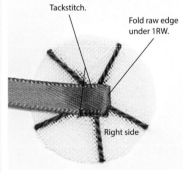

4. Thread the remaining raw edge through a tapestry needle. Twirl the needle clockwise to slightly twist the ribbon. Working counterclockwise, insert the needle under the first available spoke.

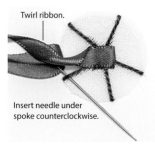

Twirl ribbon.

Insert needle under spoke counterclockwise.

5. Gently pull the ribbon under the spoke.

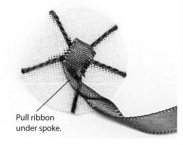

Pull ribbon under spoke.

6. Skip a spoke; thread the needle under the next spoke. Gently pull the ribbon under the spoke.

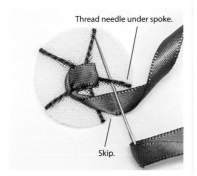

Thread needle under spoke.

Skip.

7. Continue to thread the needle over and under the spokes, pulling the center tightly and relaxing the twist as you weave around the outer spokes. Thread the needle under the last visible spoke; remove the needle. Cut off any excess ribbon, leaving a 1RW tail.

1RW tail

8. Fold the raw edge over to the crinoline. Tackstitch the raw edge to the crinoline with the threaded needle.

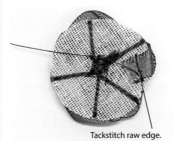

Tackstitch raw edge.

9. Tackstitch the outer petals at each spoke. Anchor knot the thread.

Tackstitch.

Finished flower

Vintage Favorite Rose Basket, 3⅛" × 2⅛"

Chou Rose in Pink, 2⅞" × 2⅜"

English Miss Rose Bowl, 1¾" diameter

Romantic Rose

Romantic Rose with Art Nouveau Leaf-M (page 119). Use same ribbon width for both flower and leaf.

SKILL LEVEL: *Intermediate* ◆◆

Suggested Ribbon

Woven or French wire ribbon with a soft or medium hand, double-sided

Amount Needed

■ Approximately 80 × width of project ribbon plus ½"*

Additional Supplies

■ 3RW crinoline circle

■ 5 folded stamens

■ Second threaded needle

Measure

Ribbon width (RW)	Measure 2RW per petal.*
1"	2"
⅞"	1¾"
¾"	1½"
⅝"	1¼"
½"	1"
⅜"	¾"

* Do not cut the ribbon until instructed to do so.

DIRECTIONS

See General Directions (page 144), Gentle Lady (page 97), and Ruched Petals (page 36).

1. Follow Step 1 for the Gentle Lady.

2. Mark 40 Ruched Petals 2RW (see chart). Anchor knot the thread at the first mark on the outer selvage edge. Follow Ruched Petals through Step 3.

3. Curve the beginning edge around the stamens. With the second needle, tackstitch the raw edge to the crinoline. Working from behind, tackstitch the first lobe to the crinoline with the next outer petal facing up.

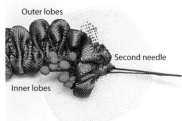

Outer lobes
Second needle
Inner lobes

4. Follow Steps 4 and 5 for the Gentle Lady, spiraling the length counterclockwise around the center. Once the petals are all stitched, smooth the petals down and away from the center.

Tackstitch inner lobes.

Finished flower

PETALS, LEAVES, AND GREENERY

Many of the flowers listed in the garden chapters have been paired with leaves to complete the designs. You will find the leaves in this chapter. The first section lists designs that can be used for a leaf or an individual petal; the second section lists designs that are specifically made to be leaves.

Leaves and Individual Petals

The following designs can be made into leaves, petals, or even buds; the only difference is the color of ribbon you chose to make the design. Any of the following techniques can be turned into a flower using the Simple Flower instructions (page 116).

PRAIRIE POINT LEAF OR PETAL ... 111
⅝" satin ribbon

PINCH TIP LEAF OR PETAL ... 113
⅜" satin ribbon

SLENDER TIP LEAF OR PETAL ... 115
⅜" satin ribbon

SOFT CURVE LEAF OR PETAL ... 111
⅜" and ⅝" satin ribbon

BOX FOLD LEAF OR PETAL ... 113
⅜" satin ribbon

MITER FOLD LEAF OR PETAL ... 115
⅝" satin ribbon

SIMPLE LEAF OR PETAL ... 112
¾" satin ribbon

ROOFTOP LEAF OR PETAL ... 114
⅜" satin ribbon

SIMPLE FLOWER ... 116
⅜" satin ribbon

LOOP LEAF OR PETAL ... 112
⅜" satin ribbon

BANDANA FOLD LEAF OR PETAL ... 114
1½" silk habotai ribbon

Leaves

The following leaf designs include both general and unique shapes, which may make them suitable for many flowers or just one in particular.

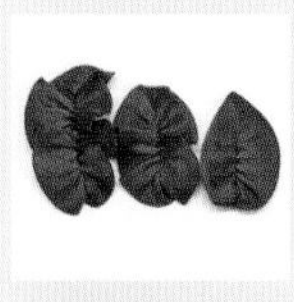

RENAISSANCE LEAF ... 117
1" silk habotai ribbon

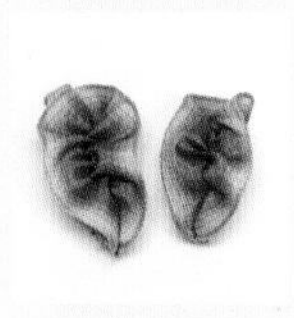

RUCHED LEAF ... 119
⅜" satin ribbon

BAROQUE LEAF ... 122
⅝" satin ribbon

SWEET LEAF ... 117
⅜" taffeta ribbon

OVAL LEAF ... 120
1" silk habotai ribbon

TUXEDO FOLD LEAF ... 122
⅞" satin ribbon

DECO LEAF ... 118
⅜" satin ribbon

NOTCHED LEAF ... 120
⅜" satin ribbon

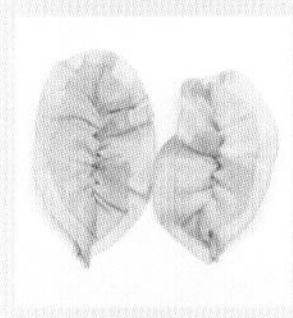

WINGED LEAF ... 123
⅝" satin ribbon

NEAPOLITAN LEAF ... 118
⅜" satin ribbon

FRILLY LEAF ... 121
1" silk habotai ribbon

HOODED LEAF ... 123
⅝" satin ribbon

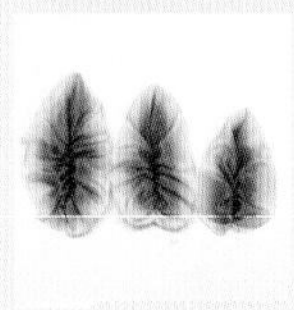

ART NOUVEAU LEAF ... 119
⅝" French wire ribbon

IVY LEAF ... 121
⅝" satin ribbon

BOW TIE LEAF ... 124
1½" silk habotai ribbon

FIGURE 8 LEAF ... 124
⅜" taffeta ribbon

GENERAL ASSEMBLY DIRECTIONS (LEAF OR PETAL)

See General Directions (page 144).

1. Follow the directions to fold, cut, loop, pin, or knot the ribbon.

2. Anchor knot the thread into the selvage edge ⅛" from the raw edge unless otherwise directed.

3. Gather stitch across the width and, if applicable, all the layers of ribbon.

4. Pull in the gathered stitches to form the bottom edge. Tackstitch through the raw edges and anchor knot the thread.

Ribbon Measurement

Each set of directions will give an RW measurement for the design. Use the Ribbon Cutting Chart (page 146) to find the correct measurement for the width of ribbon you are using.

Prairie Point Leaf or Petal

Prairie Point Leaf or Petal

SKILL LEVEL: **Easy** ◆

Suggested Ribbon

Woven or French wire ribbon with a soft, medium, or stiff hand, single- or double-sided

Ribbon Measurement
▪ 3RW

See Ribbon Cutting Chart (page 146).

DIRECTIONS

See General Assembly Directions (page 110).

1. Cut 1 length of ribbon 3RW. Fold the length of ribbon in half to find the center. Fold each side down 90°, with the raw edges resting below the selvage edge.

Insert a pin in each half through both layers of ribbon.

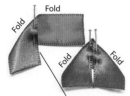

Fold below selvage edge.

2. Flip the ribbon over; anchor knot the thread into the fold. Gather stitch along the selvage edge through all the layers of ribbon. Follow Step 4 of General Assembly Directions.

Flip ribbon over.
Anchor knot.

Finished leaf or petal

Soft Curve Leaf or Petal

Soft Curve Leaf or Petal

SKILL LEVEL: **Easy** ◆

Suggested Ribbon

Woven or French wire ribbon with a soft or medium hand, single- or double-sided

Ribbon Measurement
▪ 4RW

See Ribbon Cutting Chart (page 146).

DIRECTIONS

See General Assembly Directions (page 110) and Prairie Point Leaf or Petal (at left).

1. Cut 1 length of ribbon 4RW. Follow Step 1 for the Prairie Point Leaf, overlapping the center edges slightly.

Overlap slightly.

2. Follow Steps 2–4 of General Assembly Directions.

Finished leaf or petal

Simple Leaf or Petal

Simple Leaf or Petal

SKILL LEVEL: *Easy* ◆

Suggested Ribbon

Woven or French wire ribbon with a soft or medium hand, single- or double-sided or silk bias ribbon: habotai, satin, or velvet

Ribbon Measurement
- 2RW

See Ribbon Cutting Chart (page 146).

DIRECTIONS

See General Assembly Directions (page 110).

1. Cut 1 length of ribbon 2RW. Fold the ribbon length in half, right side in, matching the raw edges. Anchor knot the thread into the selvage edges at the fold.

Stitch the selvage edges together. Anchor knot the thread.

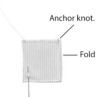

2. Open the leaf; gently poke the tip out with a stuffing tool. Follow Steps 3 and 4 of General Assembly Directions.

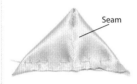

Finished leaf or petal

Loop Leaf or Petal

Loop Leaf or Petal

SKILL LEVEL: *Easy* ◆

Suggested Ribbon

Woven or French wire ribbon with a soft, medium, or stiff hand, double-sided

Ribbon Measurement
- **Short:** 4RW
- **Medium:** 6RW
- **Long:** 8RW

See Ribbon Cutting Chart (page 146).

DIRECTIONS

See General Assembly Directions (page 110).

1. Cut 1 length of ribbon. Fold the length of ribbon in half. Choose 1 of 2 variations:

- Full: Kiss the selvage edges together; pin through the raw edges.

- Tapered: Overlap the left raw edge over the right; pin through the raw edges.

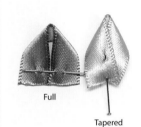

Full

Tapered

2. Follow Steps 2–4 of General Assembly Directions.

Finished leaf or petal

Pinch Tip Leaf or Petal

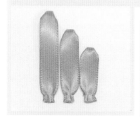

Pinch Tip Leaf or Petal

SKILL LEVEL: *Easy* ◆

Suggested Ribbon

Woven or French wire ribbon with a soft, medium, or stiff hand, single- or double-sided

Ribbon Measurement

- **Short:** 6RW

- **Medium:** 8RW

- **Long:** 10RW

See Ribbon Cutting Chart (page 146).

DIRECTIONS

See General Assembly Directions (page 110).

1. Cut 1 length of ribbon. Mark the center of the length. Fold the width of the ribbon in half, wrong side in. Tackstitch the selvage edges together at the mark. Anchor knot and cut the thread. Fold the length of ribbon in half; match and pin the raw edges.

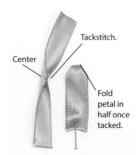

Center — Tackstitch. — Fold petal in half once tacked.

2. Follow Steps 2–4 of General Assembly Directions.

Finished leaf or petal

Box Fold Leaf or Petal

Box Fold Leaf or Petal

SKILL LEVEL: *Easy* ◆

Suggested Ribbon

Woven or French wire ribbon with a soft, medium, or stiff hand, double-sided

Ribbon Measurement

- **Short:** 6RW

- **Medium:** 8RW

- **Long:** 10RW

See Ribbon Cutting Chart (page 146).

DIRECTIONS

See General Assembly Directions (page 110).

1. Cut 1 length of ribbon. Choose 1 of 2 variations:

- Straight: Fold the length of ribbon in half; pin through the raw edges.

- Bias: Fold the length of ribbon in half on a slight bias angle; pin through the raw edges.

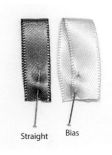

Straight — Bias

2. Follow Steps 2–4 of General Assembly Directions.

Finished leaf or petal

Rooftop Leaf or Petal

Rooftop Leaf or Petal

SKILL LEVEL: *Intermediate* ◆◆

Suggested Ribbon

Woven or French wire ribbon with a soft, medium, or stiff hand, double-sided

Ribbon Measurement

- **Short:** 4RW

- **Medium:** 5RW

- **Long:** 6RW

See Ribbon Cutting Chart (page 146).

DIRECTIONS

See General Assembly Directions (page 110).

1. Cut 1 length of ribbon. Fold the left half of the ribbon down at a 90° angle, with equal amounts of ribbon on either side of the fold. Fold the right half of the ribbon down, matching the 2 edges of the fold, the raw edges, and the selvage edges to create a point at the tip.

Fold in half at 90° angle.

Right half

Left half

Match raw edges.

2. Follow Steps 2–4 of General Assembly Directions.

Finished leaf or petal

Bandana Fold Leaf or Petal

Bandana Fold Leaf or Petal

SKILL LEVEL: *Easy* ◆

Suggested Ribbon

Silk bias ribbon: habotai, satin, or velvet

Ribbon Measurement

- 1RW

See Ribbon Cutting Chart (page 146).

DIRECTIONS

See General Assembly Directions (page 110).

1. Cut 1 length of ribbon 1RW. Fold the top right edge diagonally to the bottom left edge; finger-press the fold. Fold the top left edge diagonally to the bottom right edge; finger-press the fold. Place a pin through the raw edges.

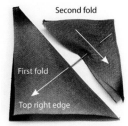

Second fold

First fold

Top right edge

Fold to bottom edge.

2. Follow Steps 2–4 of General Assembly Directions.

Finished leaf or petal

Slender Tip Leaf or Petal

Slender Tip Leaf or Petal

Suggested Ribbon

Woven or French wire ribbon with a soft, medium, or stiff hand, double-sided

Ribbon Measurement

■ **Short:** 7RW

■ **Medium:** 9RW

■ **Long:** 11RW

See Ribbon Cutting Chart (page 146).

DIRECTIONS

See General Assembly Directions (page 110) and Rooftop Leaf or Petal (page 114).

1. Cut 1 length of ribbon. Follow Step 1 for the Rooftop Leaf. Fold the width of the ribbon in half, right side in. Insert a pin 2RW from the raw edges.

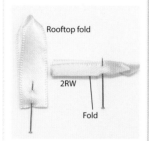

2. Anchor knot the thread into the selvage edges. Stitch diagonally toward the pin. Reverse direction and stitch back to the raw edges. Anchor knot the thread.

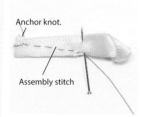

Finished leaf or petal

Miter Fold Leaf or Petal

Miter Fold Leaf or Petal

Suggested Ribbon

Woven or French wire ribbon with a soft, medium, or stiff hand, single- or double-sided

Ribbon Measurement

■ 4RW

See Ribbon Cutting Chart (page 146).

DIRECTIONS

See General Assembly Directions (page 110).

1. Cut 1 length of ribbon 4RW. Fold the length of ribbon in half. Pin 1RW from the fold.

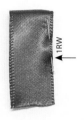

2. Fold the raw edges open. Follow Steps 2–4 of General Assembly Directions. Remove the pin.

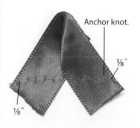

Finished leaf or petal

Simple Flower

Simple Flowers made from individual petals

 tip

Any of the individual petal designs listed in Petals, Leaves, and Greenery (page 109) can be used to create a flower.

The number of petals can be changed or the petals can be different shapes, sizes, or colors. A separate stitched center can be added; see Centers and Extra Flourishes (page 127).

DIRECTIONS

See General Directions (page 144).

Basic Construction

1. Follow the suggested ribbon and RW length given for the petal design. Cut the lengths of ribbon. Work with 1 length at a time. Follow the pin, fold, and stitch directions for the petal design.

2. Anchor knot the thread into the selvage edge of the first petal, ¼" from the raw edges. Tackstitch through each petal, above the stitched section, to join the petals together. Stitch through the selvage edge of the first petal, next to the beginning anchor knot. Gently pull the thread to form the middle of the flower.

3. **For closed center:** Insert a straw or other round object into the center of the flower. Pull in the gathers evenly, with the raw edges to

the wrong side of the flower. (At this point, stamens or a Single Knot can be added.)

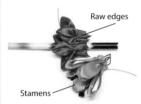

4. **For closed center:** Pull the thread tight. Tackstitch through the raw edges and anchor knot the thread.

Finished flowers

5. **For open center with flat petals:** Arrange the petals flat, with the raw edges facing in and touching. Pull the thread tight. Tackstitch and anchor knot into the raw edges.

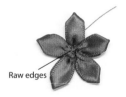

6. **For open center with flat petals:** Tackstitch a center or stitch a button into the middle of the flower to cover the raw edges.

Finished flowers

Renaissance Leaf

Renaissance Leaf

SKILL LEVEL: **Easy** ◆

Suggested Ribbon
Silk bias ribbon: habotai, satin, or velvet

Ribbon Measurement
- **Short:** 3½RW
- **Medium:** 5½RW
- **Long:** 7½RW

See Ribbon Cutting Chart (page 146).

DIRECTIONS
See General Assembly Directions (page 110).

1. Cut 1 length of ribbon. Fold and gently finger-press the width of the ribbon in half, wrong side in. Fold the length in half, matching the raw edges.

Fold

Fold Raw edges

Bias edges

2. Anchor knot the thread into the bias edges at the fold. Gather stitch through the layers of ribbon, stopping ⅛" before the raw edges. Loop over the edge and continue gather stitching up to the outer selvage edges.

Bias edges

Fold

Fold Raw edges

⅛"

Anchor knot. Loop over.

Gather stitch.

3. Gently pull in the gathers. Tackstitch and anchor knot the thread.

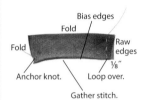

Finished leaf

Sweet Leaf

Sweet Leaf

SKILL LEVEL: **Easy** ◆

Suggested Ribbon
Woven or French wire ribbon with a soft or medium hand, single- or double-sided

Ribbon Measurement
- **Short:** 8RW
- **Medium:** 10RW

See Ribbon Cutting Chart (page 146).

DIRECTIONS
See General Assembly Directions (page 110).

1. Cut 1 length of ribbon. Fold the ribbon length in half, right side in, matching the raw edges. Anchor knot the thread into the selvage edges at the fold. Gather stitch the selvage edges together, stopping ⅛" before the raw edges.

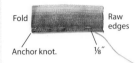

Fold Raw edges

Anchor knot. ⅛"

2. Gently pull the thread to form the leaf. Tackstitch and anchor knot the thread.

Stitch a seam to the outer selvage edge. Tackstitch and anchor knot the thread.

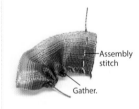

Assembly stitch

Gather.

Finished leaf

Deco Leaf

Deco Leaf

Suggested Ribbon

Woven or French wire ribbon with a soft, medium, or stiff hand, single- or double-sided

Ribbon Measurement

- **Short:** 6RW

- **Medium:** 8RW

- **Long:** 10RW

See Ribbon Cutting Chart (page 146).

DIRECTIONS

See General Assembly Directions (page 110).

1. Cut 1 length of ribbon. Fold the ribbon length in half, right side in, matching the raw edges. Insert a pin 1RW from the raw edges.

Anchor knot the thread into the selvage edges at the fold.

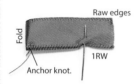

2. Stitch the selvage edges together, stopping at the pin. Stitch diagonally to the outer selvage edge, stopping ⅛" from the raw edge. Tackstitch and anchor knot the thread.

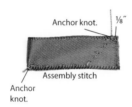

Finished leaf

Neapolitan Leaf

Neapolitan Leaf

Suggested Ribbon

Woven or French wire ribbon with a soft, medium, or stiff hand, single- or double-sided

Ribbon Measurement

- **Short:** 4RW

- **Medium:** 6RW

- **Long:** 8RW

See Ribbon Cutting Chart (page 146).

DIRECTIONS

See General Assembly Directions (page 110).

1. Cut 1 length of ribbon. Fold the ribbon length in half, right side in, matching the raw edges. Anchor knot the thread into the selvage edges at the fold.

Stitch the selvage edges together. Anchor knot the thread.

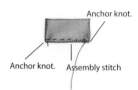

2. Open the leaf. Gently poke the tip out with a stuffing tool. Follow Steps 3 and 4 of General Assembly Directions.

Finished leaf

Art Nouveau Leaf

Art Nouveau Leaf

SKILL LEVEL: **Easy** ◆

Suggested Ribbon

Woven or French wire ribbon with a soft, medium, or stiff hand, single- or double-sided

Ribbon Measurement

- **Short:** 7RW
- **Medium:** 9RW
- **Long:** 11RW

See Ribbon Cutting Chart (page 146).

DIRECTIONS

See General Assembly Directions (page 110).

1. Cut 1 length of ribbon. Fold the ribbon length in half, right side in, matching the raw edges. Insert a pin 1RW from the fold and a second pin 1RW from the raw edges. Anchor knot the thread at the first pin.

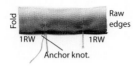

Anchor knot.

2. Gather stitch the selvage edges together, stopping at the second pin. Loop over the edges. Gather stitch at an angle to the outer selvage edge, ⅛" from the raw edge.

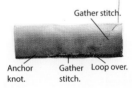

Gather stitch.

Anchor knot. Gather stitch. Loop over.

3. Gently pull in the gathers. Tackstitch and anchor knot the thread.

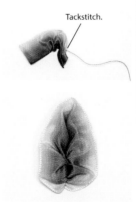

Tackstitch.

Finished leaf

Ruched Leaf

Ruched Leaf

SKILL LEVEL: **Intermediate** ◆◆

Suggested Ribbon

Woven or French wire ribbon with a soft or medium hand, single- or double-sided

Ribbon Measurement

Approximately 18 × width of project ribbon plus ½"*

See Ribbon Cutting Chart (page 146).

*Do not cut the ribbon until instructed to do so.

DIRECTIONS

See General Assembly Directions (page 110) and Ruched Petals (page 36).

1. Mark 9 Ruched Petals 2RW. Follow Steps 2 and 3 for Ruched Petals. Gently pull the thread to form the lobes of the leaf.

2. Kiss the selvage edges together. Follow Steps 2–4 of General Assembly Directions.

Start here.

Gather stitch across both widths of ribbon.

Finished leaf

Oval Leaf

Oval Leaf

Suggested Ribbon

Silk bias ribbon: habotai, satin, or velvet

Ribbon Measurement

■ **Short:** 4RW

■ **Medium:** 5RW

■ **Long:** 6RW

See Ribbon Cutting Chart (page 146).

DIRECTIONS

See General Assembly Directions (page 110).

1. Cut 1 length of ribbon. Fold the length of ribbon in half, right side in, matching the raw edges. Use assembly stitch 1 to stitch the raw edges together with a ⅛" seam.

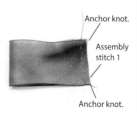

Anchor knot.

Assembly stitch 1

Anchor knot.

2. Fold and gently finger-press the length of ribbon in half. Anchor knot the thread at the seam through all the layers of ribbon. Gather stitch through all the layers of ribbon from the seam to the fold.

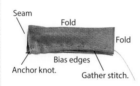

Seam

Fold

Fold

Bias edges

Anchor knot.

Gather stitch.

3. Gently pull in the gathers. Tackstitch and anchor knot the thread.

Tackstitch.

Finished leaf

Notched Leaf

Notched Leaf

Suggested Ribbon

Woven or French wire ribbon with a soft, medium, or stiff hand, double-sided.

Ribbon Measurement

■ **Medium:** 8RW

■ **Long:** 10RW

See Ribbon Cutting Chart (page 146).

DIRECTIONS

See General Assembly Directions (page 110) and Rooftop Leaf or Petal (page 114).

1. Cut 1 length of ribbon. Follow the directions for the Rooftop Leaf. Anchor knot the thread at the tip of the fold. Gather stitch through the middle of the ribbon, down the length to the raw edges.

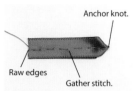

Anchor knot.

Raw edges

Gather stitch.

2. Gently pull in the gathers. Tackstitch and anchor knot the thread. Follow Steps 3 and 4 of General Assembly Directions.

Finished leaf

Frilly Leaf

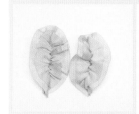

Frilly Leaf

SKILL LEVEL: *Intermediate* ◆◆

Suggested Ribbon
Silk bias habotai ribbon

Ribbon Measurement
- **Short:** 6RW
- **Medium:** 8RW

See Ribbon Cutting Chart (page 146).

DIRECTIONS
See General Assembly Directions (page 110).

1. Cut 1 length of ribbon. Fold and gently finger-press the width of the ribbon to ⅝ the original width. Fold the length in half, matching the raw edges. Insert a pin ½RW from the raw edges. Anchor knot the thread into the folded

edges at the fold. Gather stitch through all the layers of ribbon to the pin.

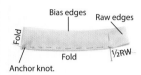

2. Gently pull in the gathers. Tackstitch and anchor knot the thread. Stitch a seam diagonally to the outer bias edges. Tackstitch and anchor knot the thread.

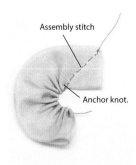

Assembly stitch

Anchor knot.

Finished leaf

Ivy Leaf

Ivy Leaf

SKILL LEVEL: *Intermediate* ◆◆

Suggested Ribbon
Woven or French wire ribbon with a soft, medium, or stiff hand, single- or double-sided

Ribbon Measurement
- Approximately 11 × width of project ribbon plus ½"*

See Ribbon Cutting Chart (page 146).

* *Do not cut the ribbon until instructed to do so.*

DIRECTIONS
See General Assembly Directions (page 110) and Boat Gather Petals (page 29).

1. Measure 3 Boat Gather Petals in this order: 3RW, 5RW, and 3RW. Follow the directions for Boat Gather

Petals through Step 3. Gently pull the thread to form the lobes of the leaf.

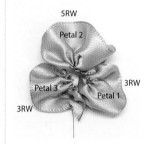

5RW

Petal 2

3RW

Petal 3

Petal 1

3RW

3RW

2. Overlap the raw edges and tackstitch the thread. Tackstitch the center of the lobes together. Anchor knot the thread.

Tackstitch center lobes.

Tackstitch raw edges.

Finished leaf

Baroque Leaf

Baroque Leaf

SKILL LEVEL: *Intermediate* ◆◆

Suggested Ribbon

Woven or French wire ribbon with a soft or medium hand, single- or double-sided

Ribbon Measurement

- 7RW

See Ribbon Cutting Chart (page 146).

DIRECTIONS

See General Assembly Directions (page 110).

1. Cut 1 length of ribbon 7RW. Fold the ribbon length in half, right side in, matching the raw edges. Fold the ribbon at an angle; pin in place. Using assembly stitch 2, stitch through the fold. Using assembly stitch 1, stitch the selvage edges together. Anchor knot the thread.

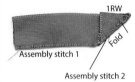

2. Open the leaf. Fold the length of the leaf in half. Tackstitch into the seam. Anchor knot the thread.

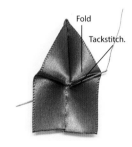

3. Follow Steps 2–4 of General Assembly Directions.

Finished leaf

Tuxedo Fold Leaf

Tuxedo Fold Leaf

SKILL LEVEL: *Easy* ◆

Suggested Ribbon

Woven or French wire ribbon with a soft, medium, or stiff hand, single- or double-sided

Ribbon Measurement

- 3RW

See Ribbon Cutting Chart (page 146).

DIRECTIONS

See General Assembly Directions (page 110) and Prairie Point Leaf or Petal (page 111).

1. Cut 1 length of ribbon 3RW. Follow Step 1 of the Prairie Point Leaf or Petal. Fold each side in a second time. Insert a pin into each side through both layers of ribbon.

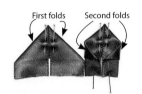

2. Gather stitch below the selvage edge through all layers of the ribbon. Follow Step 4 of General Assembly Directions.

Finished leaf

Winged Leaf

Winged Leaf

SKILL LEVEL: *Advanced* ◆◆◆

Suggested Ribbon

Woven or French wire ribbon with a soft or medium hand, double-sided

Ribbon Measurement

■ 8RW

See Ribbon Cutting Chart (page 146).

DIRECTIONS

See General Assembly Directions (page 110).

1. Cut 1 length of ribbon 8RW. Fold the ribbon at an angle; place a pin through the fold. Fold the ribbon length in half, right side in, matching the raw edges. Place a pin 1RW from the raw edges. Using assembly stitch 2, stitch diagonally toward the pin. Anchor knot the

thread at the inner selvage edge.

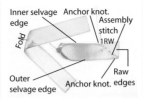

2. Stitch into the selvage edge next to the seam. Gather stitch along the selvage edge, loop over, stitch through the fold, loop over, and then continue stitching along the selvage edge.

3. Gently pull the thread to form the lobes. Tackstitch the center of the lobes together. Anchor knot the thread.

Finished leaf

Hooded Leaf

Hooded Leaf

SKILL LEVEL: *Easy* ◆

Suggested Ribbon

Woven or French wire ribbon with a soft, medium, or stiff hand, double-sided

Ribbon Measurement

■ **Short:** 4RW

■ **Medium:** 6RW

See Ribbon Cutting Chart (page 146).

DIRECTIONS

See General Assembly Directions (page 110).

1. Cut 1 length of ribbon. Fold the ribbon length in half, right side in, matching the raw edges. Anchor knot the thread into the selvage edges at the fold. Stitch the selvage edges

together. Anchor knot the thread.

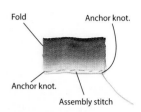

2. Open the leaf with the top curved in. Follow Steps 2–4 of General Assembly Directions.

Finished leaf

Bow Tie Leaf

Bow Tie Leaf

SKILL LEVEL: *Intermediate* ◆◆

Suggested Ribbon

Silk bias ribbon: habotai or satin

Ribbon Measurement

■ 2RW

See Ribbon Cutting Chart (page 146).

DIRECTIONS

See General Assembly Directions (page 110).

1. Cut 1 length of ribbon 2RW.

Step A. Fold the length in half and finger-press the center. Fold the top right edge diagonally to the center. Fold the bottom left edge diagonally to the center. Finger-press each fold.

Step B. Fold the bottom right edge diagonally to the center. Fold the top left edge diagonally to the center. Finger-press

each fold. Pin the edges together.

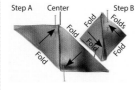

2. Anchor knot the thread in the raw edges. Following the bias and cut edges, gather stitch through all the layers, up one side and back down the other, mirroring the stitches (page 143) in the previous row.

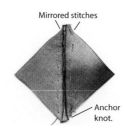

Mirrored stitches

Anchor knot.

3. Pull in the gathers to form the 2 halves of the leaf. Tackstitch and anchor knot the thread.

Tackstitch.

Finished leaf

Figure 8 Leaf

Figure 8 Leaf

SKILL LEVEL: *Easy* ◆

Suggested Ribbon

Woven or French wire ribbon with a soft or medium hand, single- or double-sided

Ribbon Measurement

■ 10RW plus ½"

See Ribbon Cutting Chart (page 146).

DIRECTIONS

See General Assembly Directions (page 110) and Gala Gather Petals (page 31).

1. Cut 1 length of ribbon. Mark 2 Gala Gather Petals 5RW each. Follow Step 2 for Gala Gather Petals. Gently

pull the thread to form the leaf.

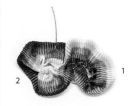

2

1

2. Match the raw edges under the middle of the leaf. Tackstitch and anchor knot the thread.

Tackstitch.

Finished leaf

Greenery

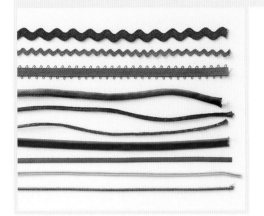

Variety of trims

Small trims such as rattail cord, silk rouleau, rickrack, or thin woven ribbons can be used for centers, stamens, or stems.

- Rayon cord is a woven cord that comes in several sizes.

- Rickrack is a woven zigzag trim that comes in several sizes.

- Satin ribbon is a woven ribbon that comes in small sizes ($\frac{1}{16}''$–$\frac{1}{8}''$).

- Silk rouleau is made from bias ribbon.

- Soutache is a flat woven braid with a channel down the center.

Cord Stem or Ribbon Stem

Primrose with cord stem

Supplies and Amount Needed
Cord or ribbon 2 × length of finished stem

DIRECTIONS
1. Cut 1 length of cord or ribbon.

2. Stitch the raw edges of the stem to the wrong side of the flower.

 tip

A calyx can be made using the directions for the Rosette (page 25) and a 6RW length of ribbon. This can be sewn or glued to the wrong side of the flower.

Wire Stem

Wire stem

Supplies and Amount Needed

- 18-gauge covered florist wire*
- ¼" satin ribbon approximately 2 × length of florist wire
- Wire cutters
- Tacky glue

If the flowers will rest in a vase, cut several different lengths longer than the height of the vase. If the flower is for a corsage and the shape will be curled, start with 1½ × the finished length of the stem.

DIRECTIONS

1. With wire cutters cut 1 length of wire. Place a dab of glue on the end of the wire. Place the raw edge of the ribbon at an angle to the wire.

2. Wrap the ribbon down at an angle, twisting the stem in the opposite direction.

3. Continue to wrap the ribbon over the wire. Place a dab of glue on the end of the wire.

4. Cut off the ribbon, leaving a ½" tail. Wrap the remaining length over the end of the wire. Pin in place until the glue dries.

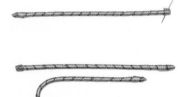

Finished wire stem, straight or shaped; glue or stitch end of covered stem to wrong side of flower

Wire Tendril

Wire tendril

Supplies and Amount Needed

- 2" of 32-gauge covered florist wire per tendril
- Stiletto

DIRECTIONS

With wire cutters cut 1 length of wire. Beginning at an end, wrap the wire over the stiletto, forming tight curls.

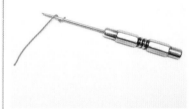

Finished wire tendril

CENTERS AND EXTRA FLOURISHES

The following designs can be used for flower centers or as separate components in a floral vignette. Most of these designs take very little yardage, so they are a great way to use those precious little bits of leftover ribbon.

SINGLE OR DOUBLE KNOT ... 128
2 colors of ⅜" satin ribbon

JELLY ROLL CENTER ... 128
⅝" satin ribbon

RUFFLED ROSETTE ... 129
⅝" satin ribbon and *Double Rosette*: ⅝" and ⅜" satin ribbon

ROSE BUD CENTER ... 130
⅝" silk satin ribbon

ROSE HIPS ... 130
2 colors of ⅜" satin ribbon

BERRY AND STUFFED BERRY ... 131
⅝" satin ribbon and 1" silk habotai ribbon

POUF GATHER CENTER ... 132
⅜" satin ribbon

STAMENS ... 132
Simple Flower with stamens

FRENCH KNOT ... 133
Rosette with French knot center

BUTTONS ... 133
Simple Flower with button

GENERAL INSTRUCTIONS

See General Directions (page 144).

These techniques may be referred to for a flower in the previous chapters. If the measurements differ, use those for the design you are constructing.

RIBBON MEASUREMENT

Each set of directions will give an RW measurement length to use in cutting, folding, or measuring the ribbon for the design. Use the Ribbon Cutting Chart (page 146) for the specific ribbon width you have selected.

Single or Double Knot

Single Knot and Double Knot

Suggested Ribbon

Woven or French wire ribbon with a soft, medium, or stiff hand, single- or double-sided

Ribbon Measurement

- **Single Knot:** 6RW

- **Double Knot:** 10RW

See Ribbon Cutting Chart (page 146).

DIRECTIONS

See General Instructions (page 127).

1. Single Knot: Cut 1 length of ribbon 6RW. Loop the right side over the left side, then up through the loop.

2. Pull the knot tight. Match the raw edges and pin together.

Finished center

3. Double Knot: Cut 1 length of ribbon 10RW. Follow Step 1; pin the left edge in place. Flip the knot over; thread the right edge through the loop again.

4. Remove the pin and adjust the lengths. Follow Step 2.

Finished center

Jelly Roll Center

Jelly Roll Center

Suggested Ribbon

Woven or French wire ribbon with a soft, medium, or stiff hand, single- or double-sided

Ribbon Measurement

- 4RW

See Ribbon Cutting Chart (page 146).

DIRECTIONS

See General Instructions (page 127).

1. Cut 1 length of ribbon 4RW. Fold the raw edges in ¼″ and finger-press in place. Fold the width in half; pin in place. Anchor knot the thread into the fold at the selvage edge.

Whipstitch the selvage edges together.

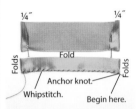

¼″   ¼″

Folds   Fold   Folds

Anchor knot.

Whipstitch.   Begin here.

2. Tightly roll the ribbon upon itself. Tackstitch the selvage edges together. Anchor knot the thread.

Tackstitch.

Finished center

Ruffled Rosette and Double Rosette

Ruffled Rosette and Double Rosette

SKILL LEVEL: *Intermediate* ◆ ◆

Suggested Ribbon

Woven ribbon with a soft or medium hand, single- or double-sided

Ribbon Measurement

▪ **Ruffled Rosette:** 8RW

▪ **Double Rosette:** 8RW in 2 different colors and widths (in same length as widest ribbon)

See Ribbon Cutting Chart (page 146).

DIRECTIONS

See General Instructions (page 127) and Rosette (page 25).

Ruffled Rosette

1. Cut 1 length of ribbon 8RW. Follow Step 1 for the Rosette using assembly stitch 1. Fold the width of the ribbon in half. Anchor knot the 2 halves together at the seam.

Seam

Anchor knot.

2. Fold the width of the ribbon in half. Follow Rosette, Step 2, stitching through both layers of ribbon. Follow Rosette, Step 3. Tackstitch and anchor knot the thread.

Seam

Folded edge

Begin here.

End here.

Finished center

Double Rosette

1. Cut 1 length of each ribbon 8RW, using the measurement of the widest ribbon. Follow the seam directions for the Rosette for each length. Cut the thread from the narrower ribbon. Turn each ribbon right side out.

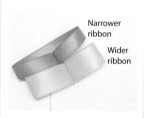

Narrower ribbon

Wider ribbon

2. Place the narrower ribbon on top, matching the seams; pin the inner selvage edges of the ribbons together. Follow the remaining directions for the Rosette. Gather stitch around the selvage edge of the wider ribbon.

Begin here.

End here.

Gather stitch.

3. Pull in the gathers just enough to pull the selvage edge under. Tackstitch and anchor knot the thread.

Tackstitch.

Finished center

Rose Bud Center

Rose Bud Center

Suggested Ribbon

Woven ribbon with a soft or medium hand, single- or double-sided

Ribbon Measurement

- Approximately 5RW*

See Ribbon Cutting Chart (page 146).

Do not cut the ribbon until instructed to do so.

DIRECTIONS

See General Instructions (page 127).

1. Measure 1RW from the selvage edge. Fold the length of ribbon behind and down at a 90° angle; place a pin through the fold. Fold the ribbon 2 more times. Measure 1RW from the last fold and cut off the excess ribbon. Fold the last petal over the first petal; pin in

place. Anchor knot the thread at the first fold.

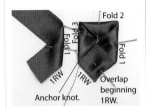

2. Gather stitch across the width of the overlapped sections. Continue around the outer edges; gather stitch back to the beginning anchor knot, looping over each corner. Cut off the excess ribbon.

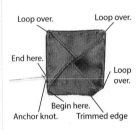

3. Pull in the gathers to form the center. Tackstitch and anchor knot the thread.

Finished center

Rose Hips

Rose Hips

Suggested Ribbon

Two-color ribbon (page 15) with a soft or medium hand, single- or double-sided

Ribbon Measurement

- 8RW

See Ribbon Cutting Chart (page 146).

DIRECTIONS

See General Instructions (page 127) and Rosette (page 25).

1. Cut 1 length of ribbon 8RW. Follow the directions for the Rosette. Beginning next to the seam, stitch

through the selvage edge of the outer ribbon. Gather stitch around the selvage edge, stopping just before the seam.

2. Pull the gathers in tightly. Tackstitch and anchor knot the thread.

Finished Rose Hips

Berry and Stuffed Berry

Berry and Stuffed Berry

SKILL LEVEL: *Easy* ◆

Suggested Ribbon

▪ **Woven Berry:** Woven or French wire ribbon with a soft or medium hand, single- or double-sided

▪ **Bias Berry:** Silk bias habotai, silk satin, or silk velvet ribbon, single- or double-sided

Ribbon Measurement

▪ **Woven Berry:** 4RW

▪ **Bias Berry:** 3RW

▪ **Stuffed (woven) Berry:** 6RW

▪ **Stuffed (bias) Berry:** 4RW

Additional Supplies

Small amount of stuffing for Stuffed Berry

See Ribbon Cutting Chart (page 146).

 note

Note that the inner selvage edge will be the top of the Berry and the outer selvage edge will be the bottom.

DIRECTIONS

See General Instructions (page 127) and Rosette (page 25). Where the directions refer to the selvage edge, that will be the bias edge for the bias ribbon.

1. Cut 1 length of ribbon. Follow the seam directions for the Rosette using assembly stitch 1. Follow the gather-stitch directions but pull the gathers so that they are formed on the wrong side of the ribbon. Anchor knot and cut the thread.

2. Turn the ribbon right side out. Anchor knot into the seam at the selvage edge. Gather stitch along the outer selvage edge back to the beginning of the seam. If you are making the Stuffed Berry, roll a small amount of stuffing into a ball and insert it into the opening.

Outer selvage edge

Outer bias edge

Stuffed Berry

3. Gently pull the thread to close the center. Tackstitch and anchor knot the thread through the selvage edges.

Tackstitch.

Tackstitch.

Stuffed Berry

Finished Berries

Finished Stuffed Berries

Pouf Gather Center

Pouf Gather Center

SKILL LEVEL: *Intermediate* ◆◆

Suggested Ribbon

Woven ribbon with a soft or medium hand, single- or double-sided

Ribbon Measurement

- Approximately 16RW plus ½"*

See Ribbon Cutting Chart (page 146).

* Do not cut the ribbon until instructed to do so.

DIRECTIONS

See General Instructions (page 127).

1. Measure ¼" from the raw edge. Mark each selvage edge (A and B). Mark 1RW from the previous mark into the center of the width of the ribbon (at C).

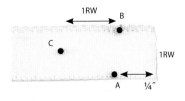

2. Continue to mark 1RW from the previous mark, alternating between the selvage edges and the center, for a total of 16 marks (8 petals). Mark ¼" from the end of the last petal. Cut the ribbon.

3. Working from behind, whip-stitch individually through mark A and then B. Straight stitch through C. This completes 1 petal. Repeat for the remaining 7 petals.

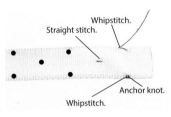

Whipstitch.
Straight stitch.
Anchor knot.
Whipstitch.

4. Pull the thread tightly to form the center, keeping the ribbon from twisting. Match the right sides of the raw edges together. Tackstitch and anchor knot the thread.

Tackstitch.

Finished center

Stamens

Stamens come in a variety of colors, shapes, and sizes and can add a realistic element to a flower.

DIRECTIONS

See General Directions (page 144).

Stamen Center

Fold the stamens in half and wrap a thin-gauge wire or thread around the folded ends to hold them together.

Stamens and Crinoline

Clip a small hole through the center of the crinoline. Insert the folded stamens through the hole. Tackstitch the stamens to the crinoline with a needle; wrap the thread several times around the stems on the wrong side.

French Knot

Large French knot centers are stitched with silk embroidery ribbon in 4mm, 7mm, or 13mm widths.

DIRECTIONS

1. Thread a chenille needle with a 12"–15" length of silk embroidery ribbon; knot the tail. Stitch the needle up through the center of the flower.

2. Hold the needle close to the flower; wrap the ribbon over the needle the number of times suggested in the chart (below). Stitch the needle down through the center of the flower.

3. Pull the needle through the wrapped ribbon to the wrong side of the flower. Knot the tail and cut the ribbon.

Rosette with large French knot

FRENCH KNOT RIBBON		
Ribbon width used in flower	Width of silk embroidery ribbon	Number of wraps
1"	13mm	7
⅞"	7mm	5
¾"	7mm	5
⅝"	7mm	3
½"	4mm	7
⁷⁄₁₆"	4mm	5
⅜"	4mm	3

Buttons

A shank or sew-through button can be stitched into the center of a flower with sewing thread, floss, perle cotton, or silk embroidery ribbon.

DIRECTIONS

Thread the needle and knot the tail. Position the button over the center of a flower. Stitch in place. Anchor knot and cut the thread or ribbon.

Simple Flower with button center

Daisy Chain, 1½" × 16"

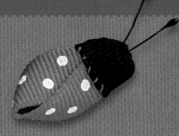

GARDEN ACCESSORIES

The following designs can be used to enhance a floral vignette, or they can be used on their own. Most of these designs take very little yardage, so they are a great way to use those precious little bits of leftover ribbon.

PRETTY LADY ... 135
⅜″ satin ribbon and ⅛″ novelty ribbon

CHERRY ... 135
⅝″ satin ribbon with
Figure 8 Leaf:
⅜″ taffeta ribbon

LADYBUG ... 136
2 colors of ⅜″ grosgrain ribbon

GRAPE BUNCH ... 136
1½″ silk bias ribbon with
Renaissance Leaf-S:
1″ silk bias ribbon

PEAPOD ... 137
⅝″ French wire ribbon and silk bias ribbon with *Sweet Leaf-S:*
⅝″ French wire ribbon

APPLE ... 138
⅝″ satin ribbon with
Soft Curve Leaf:
⅜″ satin ribbon

SNAIL ... 138
⅝″ satin ribbon

SWALLOWTAIL BUTTERFLY ... 139
⅝″ silk satin ribbon

FRILLY HEART ... 139
2 colors of ⅜″ satin ribbon

STRAWBERRY ... 140
⅝″ satin ribbon

RIBBON MEASUREMENT

Each set of directions will give an RW measurement length to use in cutting, folding, or measuring the ribbon for the design. Use the Ribbon Cutting Chart (page 146) for the specific ribbon width you have selected.

Pretty Lady

Pretty Lady

SKILL LEVEL: **Easy** ◆

Suggested Ribbon

2 different colors and widths of woven ribbon with a soft or medium hand, double-sided

Ribbon Measurement

- **Color 1:** 16RW plus ½"*
- **Color 2:** 40RW (Use ribbon ¼" narrower than Color 1.)

See Ribbon Cutting Chart (page 146).

Additional Supplies

- 2 stamens

* Do not cut the ribbon until instructed to do so.

DIRECTIONS

See General Directions (page 144) and Star Point Petals (page 33).

1. Wings: Using Color 1, mark 4 Star Point Petals in this pattern: 5RW, 3RW, 3RW, 5RW. Follow Star Point Petals; do not cut the thread.

2. Cut 1 length of Color 2 ribbon 6RW. Tie the ribbon around the center of the wings. Tackstitch the stamens to the wrong side of the wings.

Finished Pretty Lady

Cherry

Cherries with Figure 8 Leaf (page 124). Use ribbon ¼" narrower for leaf than for cherry.

SKILL LEVEL: **Easy** ◆

Suggested Ribbon

Woven ribbon with a soft or medium hand, single- or double-sided

Ribbon Measurement

- 12RW (6RW per cherry)

See Ribbon Cutting Chart (page 146).

Additional Supplies

- Small amount of stuffing
- Perle cotton #8
- Figure 8 Leaf (page 124)

DIRECTIONS

See General Directions (page 144) and Berry and Stuffed Berry (page 131).

1. Cut 1 length of ribbon 6RW. Make 1 Stuffed Berry. Tie a knot in the end of the perle cotton. Stitch the perle cotton through the center of the cherry.

2. Tie a knot close to the edge of the cherry. Cut the perle cotton to a 2" length.

3. Make 1 more cherry. Stitch 1 tail of perle cotton into the leaf. Knot the tail. Repeat for the other tail.

Finished Cherries with leaf

Ladybug

Ladybug

SKILL LEVEL: *Easy* ◆

Suggested Ribbon

2 different colors of woven ribbon in the same width with a medium hand, single- or double-sided

Ribbon Measurement

- **Body:** 4RW
- **Head:** 2RW

See Ribbon Cutting Chart (page 146).

Additional Supplies

- 1 folded stamen

DIRECTIONS

See General Directions (page 144), Loop Leaf or Petal (page 112), and Boat Gather Petals (page 29).

1. Body: Cut 1 length of ribbon 4RW. Follow Step 1 for a tapered Loop Petal.

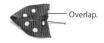

Overlap.

2. Head: Cut 1 length of ribbon 2RW. Overlap the selvage edge ⅛″ over the raw edges of the body. Whipstitch along the edge through all the layers of ribbon. Anchor knot the thread. Stitch a Boat Gather Petal, beginning and ending at the edges of the body and looping over at the outer selvage edges.

End here. Loop over.

Gather stitch.

Whipstitch.

Overlap ⅛″. Loop over.

Begin here.

3. Pull in the gathers. Anchor knot the thread. Tackstitch a folded stamen to the wrong side of the body.

Tackstitch.

Finished Ladybug

Grape Bunch

Grape Bunch with Renaissance Leaf-S (page 117). Use ribbon ½″ narrower for leaf than for grapes.

SKILL LEVEL: *Easy* ◆

Suggested Ribbon

Silk bias ribbon: habotai or satin

Ribbon Measurement

- 10RW (1RW per grape)

Additional Supplies

- Small square of crinoline

DIRECTIONS

See General Directions (page 144) and Silk Center (page 72).

1. Cut 1 length of ribbon 1RW. Follow the directions for the Silk Center. Tackstitch to a corner of the crinoline. Anchor knot and cut the thread.

2. Cut 9 more lengths; repeat Step 1 above for each remaining length. Stitch the grapes close together in rows. Trim the excess crinoline.

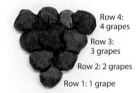

Row 4: 4 grapes

Row 3: 3 grapes

Row 2: 2 grapes

Row 1: 1 grape

Finished Grape Bunch

Peapod

Peapod with Sweet Leaf-S (page 117). Use same ribbon width for both peapod and leaf.

SKILL LEVEL: *Intermediate*

Suggested Ribbon

2 colors and types of ribbon, French wire for peas and silk bias habotai for peapod

Ribbon Measurement

▪ **Peas:** 12 × width of Color 1 ribbon

▪ **Peapod:** 4 × width of Color 2 ribbon

Additional Supplies

▪ Small amount of stuffing

▪ Second threaded needle

DIRECTIONS

See General Directions (page 144), Berry and Stuffed Berry (page 131), and Sweet Leaf (page 117).

1. Peas: Cut 3 lengths of ribbon 4RW. Make 3 Stuffed Bias Berries; do not cut the thread from the last berry. Stitch through the center of each remaining pea, leaving a pea with the finished edge on each side.

Bias edges

Finished edges

2. Stitch the needle back through each pea again, pulling the thread tight. Repeat several times. Anchor knot the thread, but do not cut it.

Anchor knot.

3. Peapod: Cut 1 length of French wire ribbon 4RW. Remove the wire from the bottom selvage edge. Using the second needle, follow the directions for the Sweet Leaf. Follow Step 2 of the Berry, gather stitching around the outer wire edge.

Gather stitch.

4. Insert the row of peas into the opening of the peapod. Anchor knot and cut the thread attached to the peas. Gently pull the remaining thread to gather the ribbon around the peas. Tackstitch the thread through the selvage edges and the group of peas. Anchor knot the thread.

Tackstitch.

Finished Peapod

Measure and Cut

Ribbon width (RW)	Peas: Color 1	Peapod: Color 2
	Cut 3 lengths 4RW.	Cut 1 length 4RW.
1"	4"	4"
⅝"	2½"	2½"

Apple

Apple with Soft Curve Leaf (page 111). Use ribbon ¼" narrower for leaf than for apple.

SKILL LEVEL: *Easy* ◆

Suggested Ribbon

Woven or French wire ribbon with a soft or medium hand, single- or double-sided

Ribbon Measurement

▪ 6RW

See Ribbon Cutting Chart (page 146).

DIRECTIONS

See General Directions (page 144).

1. Cut 1 length of ribbon 6RW. Fold the length of ribbon in half, right side in, matching the raw edges together. Anchor knot the thread into the top selvage edges, ⅛" from the raw edges. Gather stitch to the inner selvage edge.

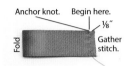

2. Loop over the edge. Continue stitching along the selvage edges through both layers of ribbon, stopping just before the fold; loop over the edge. Gather stitch up to the outer selvage edges through the fold.

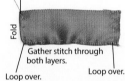

3. Gently pull the thread to form the center of the apple; bring the raw edges together. Tackstitch and anchor knot the thread.

Finished Apple

Snail

Snail

SKILL LEVEL: *Easy* ◆

Suggested Ribbon

Woven ribbon with a soft or medium hand, single- or double-sided

Ribbon Measurement

▪ Approximately 15RW plus ½"*

See Ribbon Cutting Chart (page 146).

* Do not cut the ribbon until instructed to do so.

Additional Supplies

▪ 1 folded stamen

DIRECTIONS

See General Directions (page 144) and Pincushion Center (page 80).

1. Follow Steps 1 and 2 for the Pincushion Center, pinning and stitching 15 petals. Do not cut the thread.

2. Tackstitch the folded stamen to the wrong side of the ribbon.

Finished Snail

Swallowtail Butterfly

Swallowtail Butterfly

SKILL LEVEL: *Easy* ◆

Suggested Ribbon

Woven ribbon with a soft, medium, or stiff hand, single- or double-sided

Ribbon Measurement

▪ Approximately 10RW plus ½"*

See Ribbon Cutting Chart (page 146).

* Do not cut the ribbon until instructed to do so.

Additional Supplies

▪ 2 stamens

▪ 12" of silk embroidery ribbon

▪ Chenille needle

DIRECTIONS

See General Directions (page 144) and Boat Gather Petals (page 29).

1. Mark 4 Boat Gather Petals in this pattern: 3RW and 2RW, 2RW and 3RW. Follow the directions for Boat Gather Petals. Arrange the 2 halves of the body with the wings evenly spaced.

3RW   3RW

2RW   2RW

2. Working on the wrong side, whipstitch the selvage edges together. Anchor knot the thread.

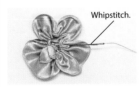

Whipstitch.

3. Tackstitch the stamen down the middle of the front of the butterfly with silk embroidery ribbon.

Tackstitch.

Finished Swallowtail Butterfly

Frilly Heart

Frilly Heart

SKILL LEVEL: *Intermediate* ◆◆

Suggested Ribbon

Two-color woven ribbon (page 15) with a soft or medium hand, double-sided

Ribbon Measurement

▪ 7RW

See Ribbon Cutting Chart (page 146).

DIRECTIONS

See General Directions (page 144) and Winged Leaf (page 123).

1. Cut 1 length of ribbon 7RW. Follow the fold directions in Step 1 for the Winged Leaf.

Anchor knot the thread ⅛" from the raw edges. Stitch the raw edges together using assembly stitch 1; anchor knot the thread.

Anchor knot.

Fold Inner edge

Assembly stitch 1

Outer edge

Begin here. Anchor knot.

2. Follow Steps 2 and 3 for the Winged Leaf.

Begin gather stitch here.

End gather stitch here.

Finished Frilly Heart

Strawberry

Strawberry

SKILL LEVEL: *Intermediate* ◆◆

Suggested Ribbon

2 colors and widths of woven ribbon with a soft or medium hand, single- or double-sided

Ribbon Measurement

▪ **Strawberry:** 2 × width of Color 1 ribbon

▪ **Calyx:** 10 × width of Color 2 ribbon plus ½"* (Use ribbon ½" narrower than Color 1.)

Additional Supplies

▪ Small amount of stuffing

DIRECTIONS

See General Directions (page 144), Simple Leaf or Petal (page 112), and Ruched Petals (page 36).

1. Strawberry: Cut 1 length of ribbon 2RW. Follow Step 1 for the Simple Leaf.

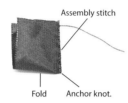

Assembly stitch

Fold   Anchor knot.

2. Open the ribbon; gently poke the tip out with a stuffing tool. Gather stitch along the raw edge; continue to the selvage edge and then along the remaining raw edge.

End here.

Begin gather stitch here.

3. Insert a small amount of stuffing into the opening. Pull the thread tight. Tackstitch and anchor knot the thread.

Tackstitch.

Finished Strawberry without calyx

4. Make a Ruched Petal Flower with 5 petals 2RW. Follow the directions for Ruched Petals. Place the calyx on top of the strawberry and tack-stitch each lobe in place. Anchor knot the thread.

Finished Strawberry with calyx

Strawberry Scissor Fob and Red Rosettes Pincushion

Measure and Cut

Ribbon width (RW)	Strawberry: Color 1	Ribbon width (RW)	Calyx: Color 2
	Cut 1 length 2RW.		Measure 2RW per petal.*
1"	2"	½"	1"
⅞"	1¾"	⅜"	¾"
¾"	1½"	¼"	½"

* Do not cut the ribbon until instructed to do so.

GETTING DOWN TO BASICS

Skill Levels

The directions for each technique are rated from beginning to advanced skill levels.

Easy ◈: All skill levels

Intermediate ◈◈: Some practice and experience required

Advanced ◈◈◈: Practice, experience, and skill required

Ribbon Basics

RIBBON YARDAGE

You will find that the majority of the projects in this book require anywhere from a few inches to a few feet of ribbon. Occasionally, a large flower will require a yard or more of ribbon. Since the length of ribbon required for a ribbonwork project depends on the width of the ribbon used, you can expect the needed lengths to vary.

To calculate the total amount of ribbon needed for a project, refer to the Amount Needed section at the beginning of each project. Simply multiply the width of the ribbon you want to use by the number given to find out the total length of ribbon required.

Glossary of Ribbon Edges

Bias edge: Unfinished edge of a bias-cut silk habotai, silk satin, or silk velvet ribbon

Folded edge: Edge created when the length or width of the ribbon is folded

Inner edge: Edge that will be gathered to create the center of the design

Outer edge: Edge that will be farthest from the center of the design

Raw edge: Cut ends of the ribbon

Ribbon length: Measurement between the cut raw edges of the ribbon

Ribbon width (RW): Measurement between the selvage or bias edges of the ribbon

Selvage edge: Finished edge of a woven ribbon

Wire edge: Finished edge of a woven ribbon that includes a thin metal wire

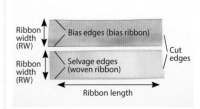

ACCURATE RIBBON MEASUREMENT

Place the ribbon on top of a ruler, with the newly trimmed raw edges aligned with the exact measurement you need. Fold, cut, mark, or pin the length of ribbon at the end of the ruler.

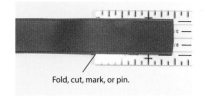

Fold, cut, mark, or pin.

Basic Hand-Sewn Stitches

Once the length is established; the ribbon is cut, folded, marked, or pinned; and the raw edges are prepared, these sections are then stitched with a variety of stitches to form, hold, or detail the shape.

ANCHOR KNOT

Use this stitch at the beginning of a row of stitches, any time the type of stitch is changed, and to finish a technique.

1. Bring the needle through the selvage or bias edges of the ribbon.

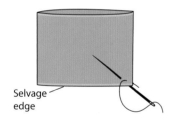

Selvage edge

2. Bring the needle through the ribbon again, inserting the needle through the loop that is created.

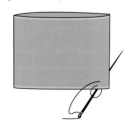

3. Tighten the knot; continue stitching or repeat the knot and cut off the thread.

ASSEMBLY STITCH 1

This is a series of short, even stitches used to stitch two sections of ribbon together to form a seam or detail.

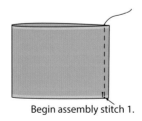

Begin assembly stitch 1.

ASSEMBLY STITCH 2

This is a series of short, even stitches used to stitch the raw edges of a seam together.

1. Begin stitching halfway up the seam toward the outer selvage edge.

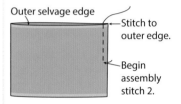

Outer selvage edge
Stitch to outer edge.
Begin assembly stitch 2.

2. Loop the thread over the selvage edge and reverse the stitches back down to the inner selvage edge. Anchor knot the thread.

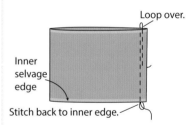

Loop over.
Inner selvage edge
Stitch back to inner edge.

GATHER STITCH

The gather stitch is a series of long, even stitches used to gather the ribbon to form a center, a petal, or the edge of a design.

Gather stitch.

GATHER STITCH VARIATIONS

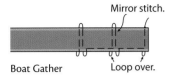

Mirror stitch.

Boat Gather   Loop over.

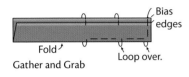

Bias edges

Fold   Loop over.

Gather and Grab

Hop 'n Stitch

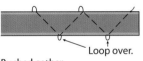

Whipstitch.

B   B

C   C

A   A

Gather stitch.

Pouf Gather

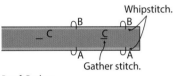

Loop over.

Ruched gather

LOOP-OVER

A loop-over stitch wraps over the selvage or bias edge of the ribbon. Use a loop-over each time you change the direction of the gather stitch in order to gather the stitches evenly. It is important that the first stitch after the loop-over maintain the same length as the previous stitches.

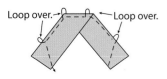

Loop over.   Loop over.

MIRRORED GATHER STITCHES

Mirrored gather stitches are two rows of gathering stitches that are stitched next to each other. The stitches should mirror each other, which will create an easier pull.

This may also be referred to as "mirroring the gather stitches."

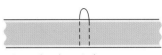

Mirrored gather stitches

TACK STITCHES

A tack stitch is a short, straight stitch that holds sections of ribbon in place, a flower to a crinoline base, or a center to a flower. The specific directions can include a grab, stab, or whipstitch.

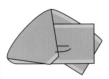

Use a grab stitch to pull an area of ribbon edge away from the rest of the design.

Use a stab stitch to tack two edges of ribbon together, or to attach the ribbon to crinoline.

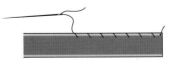

Use a whipstitch to tack two edges of ribbon together.

OUTER EDGE DETAIL STITCH

This stitch is a series of gather stitches formed on the outer edge of a design to pull in the excess ribbon and create a detailed edge.

1. Stitch through the outer layer(s) of the ribbon.

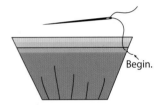

Begin.

2. Gather stitch along the edge (through both layers), ending on the wrong side.

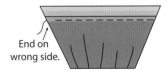

End on wrong side.

3. Pull in the gathers and anchor knot the thread on the wrong side.

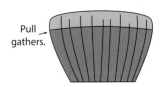

Pull gathers.

General Directions

BEFORE YOU START

- Carefully read the directions for each design. The techniques vary. The construction techniques of a design may use all or a portion of the directions from another design; follow the ribbon measurements given for your chosen design.

- Read Ribbonwork Techniques and Construction Basics (page 17) to master the vocabulary of ribbonwork.

- Read Basic Hand-Sewn Stitches (page 142) to learn the stitching techniques.

- Read Ribbons and Lace (page 12) for help choosing the right type and hand of ribbon for a particular design.

- Read Ribbon Width (page 146) to learn how to determine the length of ribbon needed.

- Read Accurate Ribbon Measurement (page 142) to learn how to measure ribbon.

PREPARATION

- Cut, fold, mark, or pin the ribbon the exact RW measurement for the design and width of ribbon you are working with.

- Prepare the ribbon so that the raw edges do not fray. See Raw Edges (page 145) for details.

- Thread a milliner's needle or small sharp with 18" of sewing thread and knot the tail. (More thread may be needed for longer lengths of ribbon.)

- If the design calls for a piece of crinoline (page 145), cut it before stitching.

STITCHING

- Sew an anchor knot (page 142) into the ribbon. Begin stitching. Anchor knot the thread any time the type of stitch changes, such as from an assembly stitch to a gather stitch.

- Remove any pins after you stitch past them.

- When gathering a continuous length of ribbon, stop when you get back to the first gather stitch; do not overlap it.

- When the directions for a layer of petals state to leave an opening in the middle of the petals for a separately stitched center, use the RW measurement of the ribbon that will be used for the center.

- A center may be added before, during, or after the flower is complete. Follow the specific directions for each flower.

- Some designs will call for two threads, one to gather and the second to tack. Follow the specific directions accordingly.

- If a design has a crinoline base, trim the base so that it does not show beyond the edges of the design.

FINISHING

- Anchor knot the thread two or three times at the end of the stitching.

- Cut off the excess thread or leave 6" of thread to sew the design to a project as necessary.

- Trim off any excess ribbon that will add bulk to the design.

- Add any French knots or buttons after the assembly is complete.

RAW EDGES

The cut edges of a woven ribbon can fray or unravel the minute the ribbon is cut. I suggest that you melt the raw edges of a synthetic woven ribbon using a thread burner tool. For a natural-fiber ribbon such as a cotton grosgrain or rayon velvet ribbon, treat the edges with a liquid fabric sealer.

Run the element of a thread burner tool down the width of each raw edge of a synthetic ribbon or melt the two edges together before they will be sewn into a seam.

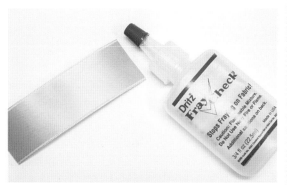

Place a small amount of liquid fabric sealer along each raw edge of a natural-fiber ribbon or place a small amount along two raw edges held together before they will be sewn into a seam.

CRINOLINE

Crinoline is a stiff, loosely woven stabilizer that is available in white and black. It is used in some cases to stabilize the petals of a flower, or as a background for several small flowers. Buckram can also be used; it is similar to crinoline but with a tighter weave.

When the directions call for a crinoline circle, the RW measurement refers to the ribbon that you are working with in the project.

To form a crinoline or buckram circle for a project that requires one, draw a square with sides equal to the RW measurement given in the design instructions. Cut out the square and then mark and trim the corners to create a circle.

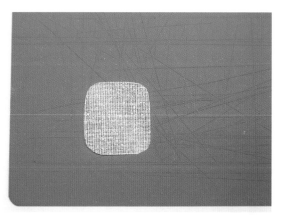

TERMS, TOOLS, AND TIPS

Spools and Tools, 8″ × 5¾″

Ribbon Width

Each dimension of a flower, leaf, center, or garden accessory is determined by the width of the ribbon used for the project. The given dimension to cut or measure is described as a multiple of the ribbon width (RW). For any project that does not include a measurement chart, refer to the Ribbon Cutting Chart for measurements up to 10RW.

To find the correct length for a width of ribbon not included in the Ribbon Cutting Chart, multiply the width of the ribbon by the RW measurement given in the project, using the Measurement Conversion Chart.

RIBBON CUTTING CHART

Ribbon width (RW)	Ribbon length								
	2RW	3RW	4RW	5RW	6RW	7RW	8RW	9RW	10RW
1″	2″	3″	4″	5″	6″	7″	8″	9″	10″
⅞″	1¾″	2⅝″	3½″	4⅜″	5¼″	6⅛″	7″	7⅞″	8¾″
¾″	1½″	2¼″	3″	3¾″	4½″	5¼″	6″	6¾″	7½″
⅝″	1¼″	1⅞″	2½″	3⅛″	3¾″	4⅜″	5″	5⅝″	6¼″
½″	1″	1½″	2″	2½″	3″	3½″	4″	4½″	5″
⁷⁄₁₆″	⅞″	1⁵⁄₁₆″	1¾″	2³⁄₁₆″	2⅝″	3¹⁄₁₆″	3½″	3¹⁵⁄₁₆″	4⅜″
⅜″	¾″	1⅛″	1½″	1⅞″	2¼″	2⅝″	3″	3⅜″	3¾″
¼″	½″	¾″	1″	1¼″	1½″	1¾″	2″	2¼″	2½″
⅛″	¼″	⅜″	½″	⅝″	¾″	⅞″	1″	1⅛″	1¼″

Toolbox Basics

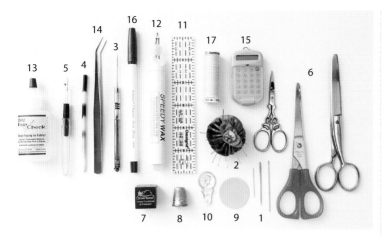

1. Needles for stitching ribbon into shape (milliner's needle or small sharp, size 10) and for embroidery using silk embroidery ribbon (chenille needles, sizes 18–24)

MEASUREMENT CONVERSION CHART	
Fraction	Decimal equivalent
1″	1″
⅞″	.875″
¾″	.75″
⅝″	.625″
½″	.5″
⅜″	.375″
¼″	.25″
⅛″	.125″
¹⁵⁄₁₆″	.9375″
¹³⁄₁₆″	.8125″
¹¹⁄₁₆″	.6875″
⁹⁄₁₆″	.5625″
⁷⁄₁₆″	.4375″
⁵⁄₁₆″	.3125″
³⁄₁₆″	.1875″
¹⁄₁₆″	.0625″

2. Pincushion

3. Knotting awl or stiletto to tuck in raw edges and wrap wire stems

4. Porcupine quill or plastic stuffing tool for adding small amounts of stuffing or forming points

5. Seam ripper

6. Several pairs of good scissors for every occasion: one for woven and silk bias ribbons, one for wire-edge ribbons, one for embroidery, and a craft pair for cutting crinoline

7. Thread Heaven (by Adam Beadworks) to condition sewing threads to minimize knotting

8. Thimble

9. Needle gripper or a pair of pliers to pull the needle through layers of ribbon

10. Needle threader

11. Clear quilter's ruler, 1″ × 6″ with ⅛″ measurements marked right to the edge

12. Speedy Wax pen or Thread Zap tool, a battery-powered tool with a heated element to prevent fraying of a synthetic-fiber ribbon by melting the raw edges

13. Fray Check (by Dritz) to keep raw edges of synthetic or natural-fiber ribbon from fraying

14. Long bent-nose tweezers for pulling ribbon right side out or tying knots in small lengths of ribbon

15. Calculator to calculate ribbon measurements

16. Invisible marker to mark a ribbon measurement

17. Good-quality sewing thread such as Gütermann polyester thread; keep on hand a wide variety of colors or several neutral colors such as gray, cream, black, red, green, and blue

Also needed (not shown in photo):

Appliqué pins to hold a fold (or ribbon edges) together

Good light source, such as an OttLite

Wire cutters to cut covered florist wire

Ribbon Care and Storage

In order for your ribbonwork designs to look their best, the ribbon you begin with should be dust- and wrinkle-free. Test the colorfastness of the ribbon if you plan to wash the finished designs.

Store your ribbon in a plastic bin and wrapped on the original cardboard spool (remove any tape that may be attached to the raw edges) or on a cardboard tube. You can also wrap the ribbon in a loop or a figure-eight bundle and store it in a plastic bag with a zipper closure. Do not secure ribbons with straight pins, as this will damage the weave; likewise, twist ties or rubber bands will leave creases.

WRINKLES

Press the ribbon only if needed. Leave the iron upright and set it on a medium-low temperature. Pass the ribbon gently over the plate. Do not press the iron directly on the ribbon; doing so will shrink silk bias ribbon, crush the pile of velvet ribbon, and potentially melt synthetic ribbon.

COLORFASTNESS

Perform a colorfastness test on silk or cotton ribbon if you plan to wash the finished piece. Place a small piece of ribbon in a cup of water for a minute or two. Take the ribbon out and lay it on a white paper towel. If the color bleeds onto the paper towel, you have two options: rinse the entire length of ribbon or make the design removable so the finished project can be washed without it.

Common Questions and Troubleshooting

What color thread should I use?

Chose a color that matches the ribbon or is slightly darker. In the photographs I used a color that would show the stitches clearly.

How do I prevent my thread from knotting?

Cut your sewing thread no longer than 18″ and condition it with Thread Heaven to eliminate tangles.

When should I knot and cut the thread?

You may ask why the thread is not always knotted and cut whenever the stitching moves to a different edge of the ribbon. The techniques are designed to minimize knotting, cutting, and re-knotting the thread because knots can be hard to hide, especially if they start at an outer edge of the ribbon.

Why doesn't my flower look like yours?

Honestly, no two flowers of mine ever look quite the same, so don't worry too much! The gather stitches may not be the same length, the ribbon might have been cut longer or shorter than the RW length, or you might have used a different ribbon than suggested. Recheck the directions, the suggested type of ribbon, and the RW.

Why is the hole in the center of my flower so big?

The gather stitches may be too short and too many; longer and fewer stitches will gather the ribbon in to make a smaller hole. Or the ribbon may be too stiff; a velvet ribbon will not gather as small as a satin ribbon. Add a large button or stitch a center from ribbon to cover the hole.

Gallery

First Blush

Candlelight and Pearls, 5½″ × 3″

A Pincushion for Constance, 4″ diameter × 2¼″ high

Bride's Choice, 3″ × 5″

Crochet Reticule with Spring Blossoms, 2¼″ × 7″

Shades of the Past

Pearl's Basket Bouquet, 3¼″ × 3¾″

Winifred's Pincushion, 3¾″ diameter × 3¼″ high

Peaches and Cream, 3⅞″ × 3¼″

Tea Dance, 11″ × 8½″

Spring in All Her Glory

Scrumptious Heart Brooch, 3½″ × 3″

China Rose Brooch, 5¼″ × 4″

Cotillion, 5¾″ × 8½″

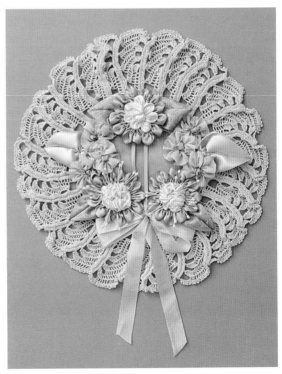

Vintage Garter with Hydrangeas and Mums, 8¾″ diameter

Sweet Nothings

Lizabeth, 5″ × 9″

Silk Roses Corsage, 3½″ × 3¼″

Tuffet of Impatiens, 2″ diameter

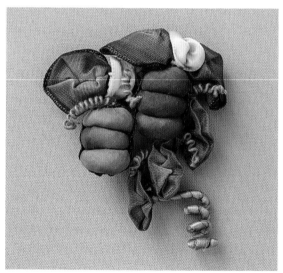

Peas in the Pod, 2½″ × 2¾″

Days of Wine and Roses

Punky Rose, 4½″ × 30″

Grand Duchess, 3¼″ × 6″

Funky Junky Steampunky, 7½″ × 3½″

Summer Place

Pretty in Pink Collar, 23½″ × 4½″

Yellow Rose of Texas, 5″ × 3¾″

Pretty in Pink Tatted Reticule, 5″ × 6½″

Clare de Lune, 3½″ × 1½″, and Silk Basket, 3¼″ × 2″

Fanciful Medley

Chou Rose in Orange, 2⅜″ diameter

Gypsy Dandelion Bouquet, 3″ × 2¾″

Persimmon Parquet, 3″ × 3″

Chantilly Ladies' Lace Cuff, 8½″ × 7⅞″

Autumn Harvest

Empress Lilies, 6″ × 6″

Straw Hat, 6⅛″ diameter

Buttons in Velvet, 4¼″ × 4″

Peapods and Roses,
7½″ × 2¼″

Vintage Echoes

Bold Stripes Brooch, 3½″ × 2¾″

Rustic Garland, 7″ × 7¼″

Burgundy Brooch, 3″ × 2⅝″

Urban Renewal, 6″ × 10⅝″

Winter's Symphony

Winter Wine, 7½″ × 9″

The Edwardian, 8¼″ × 10¼″

Geisha's Delight, 5⅜″ × 8¾″

Deco Decadence, 3″ × 5¾″

ABOUT THE AUTHOR

Photo by Kevin G. Brown

Christen Brown was born in Manhattan Beach, California, and spent her formative years in Torrance, California. She first became interested in fiber arts when she began making clothing for her dolls as a child. After graduating from high school, she continued her education at the Fashion Institute of Merchandise and Design in Los Angeles, where she graduated with an associate of arts in fashion design. She continues to be interested in craft and fine art and continues to experiment and learn about design in general, specifically in the techniques of embroidery, quilting, ribbonwork, and beadwork.

Christen began her career in the wearable art field in 1986. Her work has been shown in galleries and at fashion shows all over the world. She has been invited on multiple occasions to participate in both the Fairfield and Bernina fashion shows.

Her work has been included in *The Costume-Maker's Art, The Button Lover's Craft Book, Michaels Create! Magazine, Martha Stewart Weddings* magazine, and *Vision: Quilts of a New Decade*, to name but a few publications.

Christen is now concentrating on writing and publishing her work. Her books *Ribbonwork Gardens* and *Embroidered & Embellished* were published by C&T Publishing. She has written several articles for *PieceWork* magazine, a publication that explores the history of needlework. She has also been published in *Threads* magazine.

Christen has already had a remarkable journey through life and has set several goals for the future: to continually be inspired, to be creative, and to be necessary. She works and teaches out of her home studio in San Diego, California, and teaches several times a year locally and online. You can contact her through her website, christenbrown.com.

Previous books by Christen Brown:

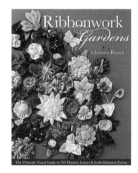
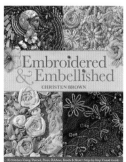

Great Titles *from* C&T PUBLISHING & stashBOOKS

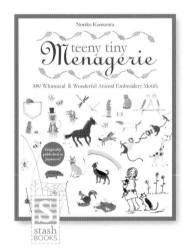

Available at your local retailer or **ctpub.com** *or* **800-284-1114**